ASIA BOND MONITOR

MARCH 2025

ASIAN DEVELOPMENT BANK

6 ADB Avenue, Mandaluyong City, 1550 Metro Manila, Philippines
Tel +63 2 8632 4444; Fax +63 2 8636 2444
www.adb.org

ISBN 978-92-9277-254-3 (print); 978-92-9277-255-0 (PDF); 978-92-9277-256-7 (e-book)
ISSN 2219-1518 (print), 2219-1526 (PDF)
Publication Stock No. SGP250107-2
DOI: http://dx.doi.org/10.22617/SGP250107-2

Note:
ADB recognizes "China" as the People's Republic of China; "Hong Kong" as Hong Kong, China; "Korea" as the Republic of Korea; "Siam" as Thailand; "Vietnam" as Viet Nam; and "Hanoi" as Ha Noi.

Cover design by Erickson Mercado.

Contents

Emerging East Asian Local Currency Bond Markets: A Regional Update

Executive Summary

Recent Developments in Financial Conditions in Emerging East Asia

A slight weakening of financial market conditions in emerging East Asia was noted from 1 December 2024 to 28 February 2025 over heightened global uncertainty surrounding economic policies and expected higher-for-longer interest rates in the United States (US).[1] While US bond yields rose for most of the review period on the Federal Reserve's less dovish stance, weaker economic data released in the second half of February pushed yields downward, particularly at the shorter end of the curve. As a result, most emerging East Asian yields fell, tracking US yield movements in February. Continued monetary easing by regional central banks contributed to the decline in yields as well.

Concerns over global trade frictions also dampened investor sentiment, resulting in portfolio outflows from the region's equity and bond markets. Foreign investors withdrew USD0.6 billion from regional equity markets from 1 December 2024 to 28 February 2025, while foreign investors pulled USD10.9 billion from regional bond markets in December–January. Five out of nine regional equity markets recorded losses and four out of seven regional markets with available data witnessed widened risk premiums. Equity markets and risk premiums in some regional economies improved, however, on supporting domestic factors. Expected higher-for-longer interest rates led emerging East Asian currencies to slightly weaken during the review period by a gross-domestic-product-weighted average of −0.9% and a simple average of −0.8%.

Risks to the region's financial conditions outlook are tilted to the downside. Shifting US economic policies could threaten both economic growth and disinflation progress in the region, as well as negatively affect investor sentiment. These impacts might also slow monetary easing in the region. The weaker-than-expected economic performance of major regional economies such as the People's Republic of China (PRC) also weighed on economic performance and investment appetite in the region. In the medium term, extreme weather events could negatively impact economic conditions and push up prices.

Recent Developments in Local Currency Bond Markets in Emerging East Asia

The emerging East Asian local currency (LCY) bond market expanded 3.1% quarter-on-quarter (q-o-q) in the fourth quarter (Q4) of 2024, compared with 2.7% q-o-q growth in the previous quarter, partly due to a lower volume of maturities for both government and corporate bonds. Outstanding government bonds rose 4.0% q-o-q to USD16.8 trillion, fueled largely by the PRC's continued issuance of sovereign debt to finance stimulus measures, albeit at less volume than in the third quarter. The region's corporate bond market grew 1.6% q-o-q to reach a size of USD8.9 trillion at the end of December, up from 0.8% q-o-q growth in the third quarter of 2024, driven by increased issuance in some markets amid lower borrowing costs. Association of Southeast Asian Nations (ASEAN) member economies' aggregate LCY bonds outstanding inched up 1.1% q-o-q to USD2.4 trillion at the end of 2024, representing a 9.2% share of the regional total.

Issuance of LCY bonds in the region totaled USD2.6 trillion in Q4 2024 on a contraction of 7.5% q-o-q due to decreased bond sales from both the public and private sectors. Government debt issuance contracted 16.3% q-o-q to USD1.1 trillion as many of the region's governments had fulfilled their borrowing requirements during the previous 3 quarters of the year. Corporate bond issuance in Q4 2024 contracted 1.2% q-o-q to USD0.9 trillion largely due to decreased corporate bond sales in the PRC amid weak growth and property market risks, which offset increased issuance in the

[1] Emerging East Asia is defined to include member states of the Association of Southeast Asian Nations plus the People's Republic of China; Hong Kong, China; and the Republic of Korea.

Republic of Korea; Hong Kong, China; and some ASEAN markets. ASEAN markets' aggregate LCY bond issuance tallied USD0.6 trillion in Q4 2024, accounting for 23.1% of the emerging East Asian total.

Outstanding Treasury bonds in emerging East Asia are predominantly long-term securities held by institutional investors. At the end of 2024, 54.0% of outstanding Treasury bonds in the region had remaining maturities longer than 5 years, while the size-weighted average tenor of outstanding Treasury bonds was 9.2 years. Banks and pension funds held an average of 34.7% and 28.9% of Treasury bonds outstanding across regional markets at the end of 2024, respectively. Meanwhile, the Treasury bond markets in Indonesia and the Republic of Korea had the region's most diversified ownership structures.

Liquidity conditions generally improved in 2024 in emerging East Asia amid easing by regional central banks. The region's government bond market saw average bid–ask spreads declining to 5.7 basis points (bps) in 2024 from 7.4 bps in 2023, while the average issue size slightly rose to USD2.2 billion from USD2.1 billion in the same period. In contrast, liquidity conditions in the corporate bond market were broadly stable. Emerging East Asian corporate bonds recorded average bid–ask spreads of 16.8 bps in 2024, roughly similar with 2023's average of 16.7 bps. The average corporate issuance size saw an increase, rising to USD84.8 million in 2024 from USD75.4 million in the previous year.

Recent Developments in ASEAN+3 Sustainable Bond Markets

At the end of 2024, sustainable bonds outstanding in ASEAN+3 markets totaled USD917.6 billion, with growth moderating to 12.1% year-on-year (y-o-y) from 29.4% y-o-y in 2023 amid a slowdown in issuance. The slower pace of growth in ASEAN+3's sustainable bond market largely tracked the growth moderation in the global market from 22.2% y-o-y in 2023 to 15.2% y-o-y in 2024. Nonetheless, ASEAN+3 remained the world's second-largest sustainable bond market with a global share of 18.9%, following the European Union 20's (EU-20) share of 36.6%. ASEAN+3's sustainable bond market, however, remains relatively small, equivalent to only 2.3% of its general bond market, compared with 8.1% in the EU-20.

Issuance of sustainable bonds in ASEAN+3 tallied USD237.2 billion during 2024, posting a 3.1% y-o-y contraction due to elevated interest rates and expectations of policy shifts in the US. Despite the slowdown, ASEAN+3 outperformed the EU-20, whose sustainable bond issuance contracted 9.0% y-o-y. Both the EU-20 and ASEAN+3 maintained their status in 2024 as the world's two largest markets in terms of sustainable bond issuance, with global shares of 30.2% and 25.2%, respectively. The decline in ASEAN+3's sustainable bond issuance in 2024 was led by a 21.8% y-o-y fall in green bond issuance. While ASEAN+3's sustainable bond issuance was predominantly in LCY (75.5%), it lagged the LCY share in the region's general bond market (95.6%). In contrast, the EU-20's LCY shares in its sustainable bond (86.6%) and general bond (78.0%) markets were roughly comparable. In terms of issuer profile, the private sector accounted for 65.1% of sustainable bond issuance in ASEAN+3 in 2024. Around 73.0% of 2024 sustainable bond issuances in ASEAN+3 carried tenors of 5 years or less, with a size-weighted average tenor of 6.0 years, which is less than the corresponding average of 9.0 years in the EU-20. In ASEAN markets, 56.5% of sustainable bond issuances in 2024 carried tenors longer than 5 years, with a size-weighted-average tenor of 12.3 years, largely due to public sector issuance.

Developments in Regional Financial Conditions

Financial conditions in emerging East Asia slightly weakened between 1 December 2024 and 28 February 2025 amid heightened global uncertainty and higher-for-longer United States (US) interest rates.[1] Bond yields mostly rose in advanced economies as inflation remained persistent during the review period, leading to slower-than-expected rate cuts by the US Federal Reserve (**Table A**). Higher-for-longer interest rates in the US slightly weighed on regional currencies during the review period. Most bond yields in the region declined, tracking US movements, amid continued monetary easing in the region. Uncertainty regarding US trade policies and their possible impact on major US trading partners in emerging East Asia have dampened investor sentiment, leading to portfolio outflows from regional equity and bond markets, and equity losses and widened risk premiums in the majority of regional markets. Nevertheless, favorable domestic factors supported investor sentiment in some regional markets, leading to equity gains and narrowed risk premiums in those markets.

In advanced economies, yields rose during the review period for the 10-year tenor. In both the US and the euro area, long-term yield upticks were driven by elevated inflation as well as ongoing uncertainties in US economic policy, while yield gains in Japan followed its central bank's monetary tightening.

From 1 December 2024 to 14 February 2025, the US saw a rise in both its 2-year and 10-year bond yields amid sound economic performance and persistent inflation. Gross domestic product (GDP) growth remained solid in the fourth quarter (Q4) of 2024 at an annualized 2.3%, leaving full-year 2024 GDP growth at a robust 2.8%. Domestic consumption continued to post strong gains,

Table A: Changes in Financial Conditions in Major Advanced Economies and Select Emerging East Asian Markets from 1 December 2024 to 28 February 2025

	2-Year Government Bond Yield (bps)	10-Year Government Bond Yield (bps)	5-Year Credit Default Swap Spread (bps)	Equity Index (%)	FX Rate (%)
Major Advanced Economies					
Euro Area	7	32	–	13.7	(1.9)
Japan	22	33	(6)	0.04	(0.6)
United States	(16)	4	–	(1.3)	–
Select Emerging East Asian Markets					
People's Republic of China	8	(26)	(17)	(0.2)	(0.4)
Hong Kong, China	(8)	30	–	18.1	0.04
Indonesia	(11)	(5)	4	(11.9)	(4.4)
Republic of Korea	(2)	(6)	(5)	3.1	(4.3)
Malaysia	(1)	(1)	2	(1.2)	(0.3)
Philippines	(11)	13	4	(9.3)	1.1
Singapore	(13)	(0.5)	–	4.2	(0.9)
Thailand	(9)	(15)	4	(15.7)	0.4
Viet Nam	25	33	(5)	4.4	(0.8)

( ) = negative, – = not available, bps = basis points, FX = foreign exchange.

Note: FX rates are presented against the United States dollar. A positive (negative) value for the FX rate indicates the appreciation (depreciation) of the local currency against the United States dollar.

Source: *AsianBondsOnline* calculations based on Bloomberg LP data.

[1] Emerging East Asia is defined to include member states of the Association of Southeast Asian Nations plus the People's Republic of China; Hong Kong, China; and the Republic of Korea.

rising an annualized 4.2% in Q4 2024 after gaining 3.7% in the previous quarter. The S&P Global US manufacturing Purchasing Managers Index (PMI) continued to rise in expansionary territory, reaching 52.7 in February from 51.2 in January and 49.4 in December. This uptick was largely supported by increased output and new orders. Meanwhile, the unemployment rate slightly rose to 4.1% in February from 4.0% in January but was unchanged from December's 4.1%. Nonfarm payrolls weakened in February and January to 151,000 and 125,000, respectively, from 323,000 in December. At its December meeting, the Federal Reserve revised its GDP forecast for 2025 upward to 2.1% from 2.0% in September, while the corresponding forecast for the unemployment rate was revised down to 4.3% from 4.4%. However, more recent economic indicators have shown some weakness, leading the Federal Reserve to downgrade its 2025 GDP forecast in March to 1.7%, while it revised the unemployment rate up to 4.4%.

The release of several weaker data indicators in the second half of February contributed to the overall fall in the 2-year yield during the review period. Retail sales contracted 1.2% month-on-month (m-o-m) in January after a 0.7% m-o-m gain each in December and November, posting the largest decline since April 2023. The consumer confidence index fell steeply to 98.3 in February from 105.3 in January and 109.5 in December.

Meanwhile, inflationary pressure in the US economy persists. Consumer price inflation remains above the Federal Reserve's 2.0% target at 2.8% year-on-year (y-o-y) in February from 3.0% y-o-y in January and 2.9% y-o-y in December. Core inflation ticked down to 3.1% y-o-y in February from 3.3% y-o-y in January and 3.2% y-o-y in December. In January, however, personal consumption expenditures (PCE) inflation inched back down to 2.5% y-o-y from 2.6% y-o-y in December and 2.5% y-o-y in November, while core PCE inflation fell to 2.6% y-o-y in January from 2.9% y-o-y in December, following a slight uptick from 2.8% y-o-y in November, which was in line with Federal Reserve projections. In December, the Federal Reserve revised upward its 2025 projection for PCE inflation to 2.5% from 2.1% and for core PCE inflation to 2.5% from 2.2%. Further, in March, the Federal Reserve raised its PCE inflation and core PCE inflation forecasts for 2025 to 2.7% y-o-y and 2.8% y-o-y, respectively.

Persistent inflationary pressure and heightened uncertainty over economic policies have led the Federal Reserve to become less dovish. While the Federal Reserve reduced the target rate range by 25 basis points (bps) during its 17–18 December 2024 Federal Open Market Committee (FOMC) meeting, the number of projected rate cuts in 2025 was reduced to two from a forecast of four made in September. The release of the December FOMC meeting minutes on 8 January indicated increased upside risks for inflation following the uptick in inflation data and uncertainty regarding future economic policies. In December and January, Federal Reserve officials expressed caution over the inflation path and uncertainty over US policy shifts. As was widely expected, the Federal Reserve left its target rate range unchanged at 4.25%–4.50% at its 28–29 January FOMC meeting. The Federal Reserve removed the phrase regarding progress toward inflation from its monetary policy statement, indicating rising uncertainty. During the January FOMC press conference, Federal Reserve Chair Jerome Powell indicated that he would like to see further progress on inflation before adjusting interest rates. On 12 February, Jerome Powell testified to Congress that they were not in a hurry to adjust policy rates.

Despite some softer economic indicators released in February, other Federal Reserve officials also remained cautious over inflationary pressure, casting uncertainty on the monetary easing path. Federal Reserve Bank of Richmond President Thomas Barkin on 25 February said that he expected January PCE inflation to be lower but noted that it still makes sense for monetary policy to stay moderately restrictive. On 27 February, Federal Reserve Bank of Atlanta President Raphael Bostic also said that the Federal Reserve needed to stay restrictive. As widely expected, the Federal Reserve left its policy rate unchanged at its 18-19 March FOMC meeting. Based on the CME FedWatch Tool, as of 28 February, the likelihood of a cumulative 50 bps rate reduction (via two rate cuts) in 2025 rose to 27.6% from 22.7% as of 2 December, while the probability for a 75 bps reduction (via three rate cuts) rose to 31.8% from 28.8% (**Figure A**).

In the euro area, yields rose during the review period, tracking persistent inflation, despite continued easing by the European Central Bank (ECB). Economic indicators in the euro area remain subdued. GDP in the euro area grew 1.2% y-o-y in Q4 2024, up from 1.0% y-o-y in the third quarter (Q3) of 2024. However, on a quarter-on-quarter (q-o-q) basis, GDP growth decelerated to 0.2% in Q4 2024 from 0.4% in Q3 2024. The manufacturing PMI reading, which has remained in contractionary territory since July 2022, rose slightly to 47.6 in February from 46.6 in January 2025, a 2-year high. During its December

Figure A: Probability of Cumulative Rate Adjustments by the Federal Reserve in 2025

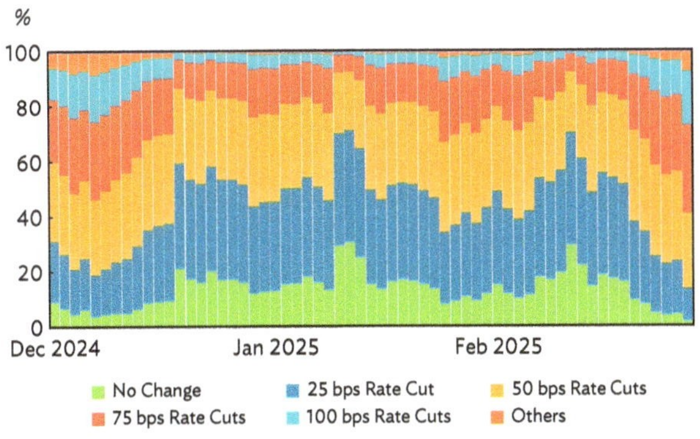

bps = basis points.
Note: Data are as of 28 February 2025.
Source: CME FedWatch Tool.

meeting, the ECB revised downward its GDP forecasts for 2025 and 2026 to 1.1% and 1.4%, respectively, from September forecasts of 1.3% and 1.5%. Subsequently, the ECB further downgraded the GDP outlook for 2025 and 2026 to 0.9% and 1.2%, respectively, in March. Inflation in the euro area slightly eased to 2.3% y-o-y in February after ticking up to 2.5% y-o-y in January 2025 from 2.4% y-o-y in December. The ECB noted that the uptick in inflation in December was expected and acknowledged that near-term inflation may fluctuate around current levels, as both domestic and service inflation are still persistently high. However, the ECB also expects consumer price inflation to fall and eventually reach its 2.0% target over the medium term. During its December meeting, the ECB revised downward its consumer price inflation forecast for full-year 2025 to 2.1% from a 2.2% forecast made in September, while keeping its 2026 inflation forecast unchanged at 1.9%. The inflation forecast for 2025, however, was subsequently revised upward to 2.3% during its March meeting.

The ECB's monetary easing remained on track during the review period, but concerns were elevated over increased global uncertainty. To support economic growth, the ECB consecutively reduced its key policy rates—the deposit facility, main refinancing operations, and marginal lending facility—by 25 bps each at its 12 December, 30 January, and 6 March monetary policy meetings, citing that the disinflation process remained on track and economic growth was expected to remain weak in the near-term. Nevertheless, ECB officials, while supporting rate cuts, have turned cautious over rising global volatility.[2] On 11 February, ECB President Christine Lagarde noted that while the disinflation trend was on track, greater friction in trade could add to inflation uncertainty. On 12 February, ECB Executive Board Member Frank Elderson said that in light of elevated global volatility, it was important to examine its impact on inflation. On the same day, ECB Governing Council Member Joachim Nagel noted the importance of not acting hastily in the present uncertain environment.

Monetary tightening by the Bank of Japan (BOJ), amid an expected economic recovery and rising inflation, drove yields up during the review period. However, Japan's economic performance remained subdued. While Japan's GDP recorded annualized 2.2% growth in Q4 2024 after gaining 1.4% in Q3 2024, full-year GDP growth was only 0.1% in 2024 versus 1.5% in 2023. Domestic consumption was weak in Q4 2024, unchanged from Q3 2024. Industrial production, however, gained 2.2% y-o-y in January after falling 2.2% y-o-y in December. Manufacturing PMI remained weak but improved somewhat to 49.0 in February from 48.7 in January. Inflation in Japan remained elevated at 3.7% y-o-y in February, down slightly from 4.0% y-o-y in January but still up from 3.6% y-o-y in December. Meanwhile, the unemployment rate stood at 2.5% y-o-y in January, higher than December's 2.4% figure but unchanged from November's.

During its 19 December 2024 meeting, the BOJ left its policy rate unchanged but noted that the domestic economy is recovering and expected to grow above potential. The central bank also acknowledged that consumer price inflation is expected to rise. The BOJ later raised its key policy rate by 25 bps at its 24 January 2025 meeting, noting that if current projections were met, the BOJ would implement additional rate hikes. The BOJ released updated economic forecasts in January, keeping GDP forecasts for 2025 (1.1%) and 2026 (1.0%) unchanged from those made in October, while revising consumer price inflation projections upward for 2025 and 2026 to 2.4% y-o-y and 2.0% y-o-y, respectively, from October projections of 1.9% y-o-y and 1.9% y-o-y. BOJ Governor Kazuo Ueda on 12 February said that the recent rise in food prices could have an impact on inflation expectations. On 19 March, the BOJ left its policy rate unchanged at 0.5%.

[2] These include talks given by Bank of France Governor Francois Villeroy de Galhau, ECB Executive Board Member Philip Lane, Bank of Austria Governor Robert Holzmann, Bank of Lithuania Governor Gediminas Simkus, and National Bank of Slovakia Governor Peter Kazimir.

In emerging East Asia, local currency government bond yields declined for most markets, largely driven by the easing stances of central banks in the region. Bond yields declined for both 2-year and 10-year maturities in Indonesia, the Republic of Korea, Singapore, and Thailand following monetary policy easing by their respective central banks during the review period. In contrast, Viet Nam's yields rose on strong growth expectations as the government revised upward its GDP growth forecast for 2025. Meanwhile, the People's Republic of China (PRC) saw a significant decline in its 10-year yield during the review period amid low inflation and the central bank's easing monetary stance. The PRC had the region's lowest inflation rate, falling to −0.7% y-o-y in February from January (0.5% y-o-y) on weak domestic demand (**Figure B**). The People's Bank of China announced it would ease its monetary policy further sometime this year.

Several regional central banks continued their monetary easing to support economic growth amid heightened uncertainty:

- After having left policy rates unchanged in Q4 2024, Bank Indonesia reduced its key rate by 25 bps on 15 January, in line with benign domestic inflation as well as to support economic growth. Bank Indonesia left policy rates unchanged in its subsequent meetings in February and March, citing high global uncertainty over the implementation of US import tariffs and the Federal Reserve's policy stance (**Table B**).
- On 24 January, the Monetary Authority of Singapore reduced slightly the slope of the Singapore dollar nominal effective exchange rate, reflecting its easing stance, noting that economic growth had moderated and inflation had fallen much more quickly than expected.
- The Bank of Korea left monetary policy unchanged during its 16 January meeting amid increased volatility in exchange rates and uncertainty in the economic outlook. The central bank subsequently cut its policy rate by 25 bps at its meeting on 25 February, noting that economic growth is expected to slow and the global economy faces downward pressure.
- In the Philippines, the Bangko Sentral ng Pilipinas (BSP) left the policy rate unchanged in its 13 February meeting after it reduced the policy rate by 25 bps in both October and December. The BSP noted that while the inflation outlook has not substantially changed, there are increased price pressures in the utilities sector and uncertainty over the impact of foreign economic policies on the domestic economy. On 5 February, BSP Governor Eli Remolona said that a cumulative 50 bps rate cut for 2025 was possible—scaling back his November outlook of a cumulative 100 bps rate cut for 2025. However, on 21 February, the BSP announced cuts to its reserve requirement ratio for banks and nonbank financial institutions by 200 bps effective 28 March.
- The Bank of Thailand reduced policy rates on 26 February, as the economy is expected to slow.
- The People's Bank of China, which last reduced policy rates in September 2024, indicated on 4 January that it intended to continue with its moderately loose monetary policy by lowering policy rates and reserve requirement ratios later this year.

Figure B: Inflation in Major Advanced Economies and Select Emerging East Asian Markets

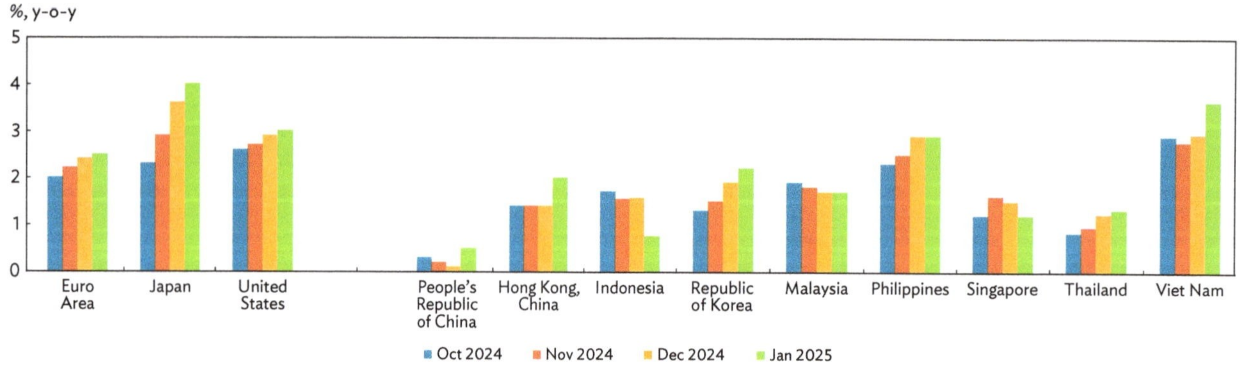

y-o-y = year-on-year.

Sources: Various local sources.

Table B: Changes in Monetary Stances in Major Advanced Economies and Select Emerging East Asian Markets

Economy	Policy Rate 1-Feb-2024 (%)	Rate Change (%) Feb-2024	Mar-2024	Apr-2024	May-2024	Jun-2024	Jul-2024	Aug-2024	Sep-2024	Oct-2024	Nov-2024	Dec-2024	Jan-2025	Feb-2025	Policy Rate 28-Feb-2025 (%)	Change in Policy Rates (basis points)
Euro Area	4.00					↓0.25			↓0.25	↓0.25		↓0.25		↓0.25	2.75	↓ 125
Japan	(0.10)		↑0.20				↑0.15						↑0.25		0.50	↑ 60
United Kingdom	5.25							↓0.25			↓0.25			↓0.25	4.50	↓ 75
United States	5.50								↓0.50		↓0.25	↓0.25			4.50	↓ 100
People's Republic of China	1.80						↓0.10		↓0.20						1.50	↓ 30
Indonesia	6.00			↑0.25					↓0.25				↓0.25		5.75	↓ 25
Republic of Korea	3.50									↓0.25	↓0.25			↓0.25	2.75	↓ 75
Malaysia	3.00														3.00	◆ 0
Philippines	6.50							↓0.25		↓0.25		↓0.25			5.75	↓ 75
Singapore	–												↓		–	↓ –
Thailand	2.50									↓0.25				↓0.25	2.00	↓ 50
Viet Nam	4.50														4.50	◆ 0

( ) = negative, ◆ = no change, – = no data.

Notes:
1. Data coverage is from 1 February 2024 to 28 February 2025.
2. For the People's Republic of China, the data used in the chart is for the 7-day reverse repurchase rate.
3. For the United States, the upper bound of the policy rate target range is reported on the table.
4. The up (down) arrow for Singapore signifies monetary policy tightening (loosening) by its central bank. The Monetary Authority of Singapore utilizes the Singapore dollar nominal effective exchange rate to guide its monetary policy.

Sources: Various central bank websites.

- Bank Negara Malaysia, on 6 March, left its monetary policy unchanged, noting that the decision was in line with the favorable domestic economic growth and inflation outlooks. However, the central bank noted that there was elevated global policy uncertainty, which could create greater volatility.

Economic growth in the region remained solid in Q4 2024, with most markets posting faster growth compared to the previous quarter. Among regional markets, Viet Nam posted its most rapid growth since Q3 2022 and the highest in the region at 7.6% y-o-y, buoyed by domestic consumption, exports, and investments (**Table C**). GDP growth in the PRC accelerated over the same period to 5.4% y-o-y from 4.6% y-o-y, supported by stimulus measures. Meanwhile, economic performances in the Republic of Korea and Singapore slowed when compared with the previous quarter. In the Republic of Korea, economic growth moderated over weak consumption, a slowdown in export growth, and a continued contraction in investments, while in Singapore it was due to slower growth in manufacturing. Based on the *Asian Development Outlook December 2024*, the most recent 2025 growth projections for East Asia and Southeast Asia were unchanged from September estimates of 4.2% and 4.7%, respectively.

Table C: Gross Domestic Product Growth in Select Emerging East Asian Economies (y-o-y, %)

Economy	2024 Q1	Q2	Q3	Q4	Full Year	Forecast for 2025
PRC	5.30	4.70	4.60	5.40	5.00	4.50
HKG	2.80	3.10	1.90	2.40	2.50	2.30
INO	5.11	5.05	4.95	5.02	5.03	5.00
KOR	3.30	2.30	1.50	1.20	2.00	2.00
MAL	4.20	5.90	5.40	5.00	5.10	4.60
PHI	5.80	6.40	5.24	5.23	5.60	6.20
SIN	3.20	3.40	5.70	5.00	4.40	2.60
THA	1.70	2.30	3.00	3.20	2.50	2.70
VIE	5.66	6.93	7.43	7.55	7.09	6.60

PRC = People's Republic of China; HKG = Hong Kong, China; INO = Indonesia; KOR = Republic of Korea; MAL = Malaysia; PHI = Philippines; Q1 = first quarter; Q2 = second quarter; Q3 = third quarter; Q4 = fourth quarter; SIN = Singapore; THA = Thailand; VIE = Viet Nam; y-o-y = year-on-year.

Note: Forecasts for 2025 are based on the *Asian Development Outlook* December 2024.

Sources: Various local sources.

However, growth forecasts were revised down for both Hong Kong, China (from 3.0% to 2.3%) and the Republic of Korea (from 2.3% to 2.0%).

Amid expected higher-for-longer interest rates in the US, emerging East Asian currencies marginally weakened during the review period, depreciating 0.9% (GDP-weighted) and 0.8% (simple average) versus the US dollar. Projections from the Federal Reserve in December showing fewer expected rate cuts in 2025 than previously anticipated, as well as more cautious language from Federal Reserve officials regarding inflation, led to the broad strengthening of the US dollar. Uncertainties regarding the impact of US tariffs on regional economic growth placed added downward pressure on currencies. During the review period, the Indonesian rupiah fell the most in the region (–4.4%) over domestic fiscal concerns. The Korean won fell 4.3% largely due to ongoing domestic political issues (**Figure C**). On the other hand, the Philippine peso gained 1.1% during the review period as the BSP indicated that it expects to implement fewer rate cuts this year than previously expected.

Figure C: Currency Exchange Rates Against the United States Dollar in Select Emerging East Asian Markets

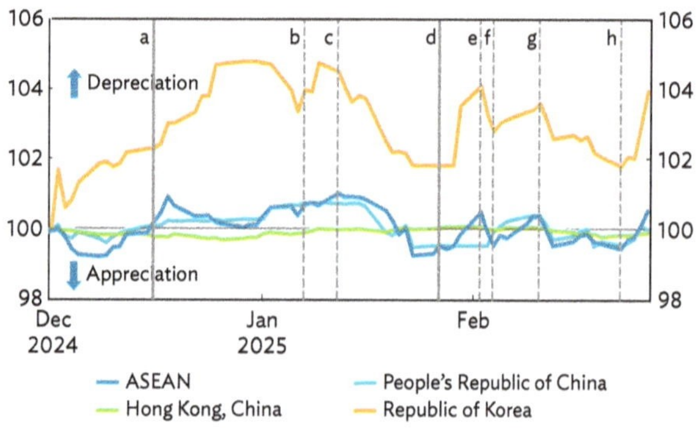

ASEAN = Association of Southeast Asian Nations, US = United States.

Notes:

1. Corresponding dates of the following news reported:
   - a The Federal Reserve lowered the federal funds rate by 25 basis points to a range of 4.25%–4.50%, but it also suggested a slower pace of rate cuts in 2025.
   - b The December Federal Open Market Committee meeting minutes included members noting that upside risks to inflation had increased and the Federal Reserve would move slowly on rate cuts.
   - c Plans for the gradual implementation of tariffs by the United States are reported.
   - d The Federal Reserve maintained its interest rates within a range of 4.25%–4.50% amid elevated inflation and stable labor market conditions.
   - e US delays implementation of tariffs on goods from Mexico and Canada.
   - f Federal Reserve officials (Austan Goolsbee and Thomas Barkin) noted rising uncertainty due to possible shifts in US economic policy.
   - g The possible delay of tariff implementation to April due to reciprocal tariff investigations is reported.
   - h US tariffs on Canada and Mexico are scheduled to proceed in March.
2. ASEAN comprises the markets of Indonesia, Malaysia, the Philippines, Singapore, Thailand, and Viet Nam.
3. Data are as of 28 February 2025.
4. A value higher (lower) than 100 indicates currency depreciation (appreciation) against the US dollar.

Source: *AsianBondsOnline* calculations based on Bloomberg LP data.

Heightened economic policy uncertainty contributed to portfolio outflows from the region during the review period. Regional equity markets logged net portfolio outflows of USD0.6 billion from 1 December 2024 to 28 February 2025, with net portfolio outflows observed in all regional markets totaling USD6.7 billion in December and USD3.3 billion in January (**Figure D**). In February, the region excluding the PRC continued to record net outflows of USD4.7 billion, however, net inflows in the PRC (USD14.0 billion) drove the region's net portfolio inflows of USD9.4 billion during the month. The net inflows in the PRC in February were mostly driven by new measures announced on 13 January to implement funding facilities aimed at supporting stock purchases.[3] Further measures were announced on 22 January to help stabilize the PRC's stock market.[4] Meanwhile, the Republic of Korea continued to post outflows (USD2.8 billion) in February as investor sentiment was dragged down by lingering domestic political concerns.

Most bond markets in the region also posted net outflows during the review period. Between 1 December and 31 January, the regional bond market recorded net

Figure D: Foreign Capital Flows in Select Emerging East Asian Equity Markets

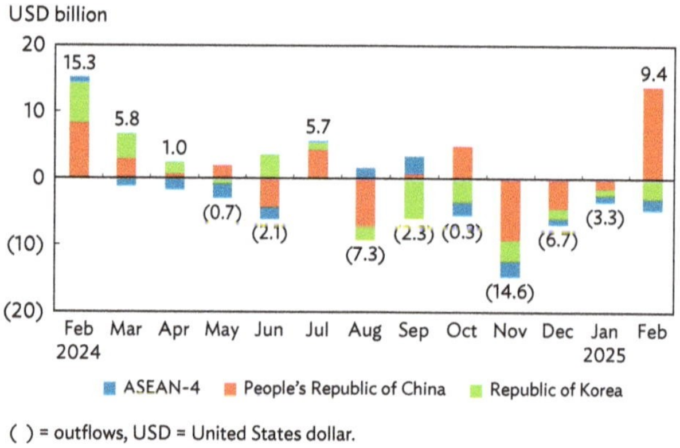

( ) = outflows, USD = United States dollar.

Notes:

1. Data coverage is from 1 February 2024 to 28 February 2025.
2. The numbers above (below) each bar refer to net inflows (net outflows) for each month.
3. Emerging East Asia is defined to include member states of the Association of Southeast Asian Nations (ASEAN) plus the People's Republic of China; Hong Kong, China; and the Republic of Korea.
4. ASEAN-4 includes Indonesia, the Philippines, Thailand, and Viet Nam.

Source: Institute of International Finance.

[3] In January, the China Securities Regulatory Commission announced plans to help boost the stock market. Among others, these include collaboration with the central bank to provide funding facilities for stock repurchases, encouraging companies to increase their dividend payouts and small investor protection through special litigation, and expanded efforts to combat financial fraud.

[4] The measures include (i) encouraging mutual funds to create more equity-related investment products; (ii) expanding listed corporates access to the relending tool of the central bank; (iii) allowing mutual funds and insurance companies to increase their stock market investments; and (iv) making adjustments to the performance appraisal of state-owned insurers, among others.

outflows of USD10.9 billion. Investor sentiment was negatively affected by persistent inflation in the US and the less dovish stance taken by Federal Reserve officials since December. The region's bond market saw net outflows of USD4.7 billion in December, followed by additional outflows of USD6.1 billion in January, resulting in 5 straight months of net outflows from September 2024 through January 2025 (**Figure E**). The largest outflows between 1 December and 31 January were recorded in the PRC (USD8.1 billion), over concerns about economic performance, and in the Republic of Korea (USD2.8 billion), on heightened political uncertainty.

Five out of nine equity markets in the region weakened during the review period as uncertainty over US economic policy and monetary policy dampened investor sentiment. The region recorded a simple average loss of –0.9% during the review period but a market-weighted average gain of 3.3% that was driven by equity rallies in Hong Kong, China; Viet Nam; and Singapore. The largest gains were recorded in Hong Kong, China (18.1%), buoyed by technology stocks' rally over artificial intelligence (AI) innovations such as DeepSeek (**Figure F**). A discussion on how AI can be beneficial for the financial industry but could also pose challenges is discussed in **Box 1**. The next largest equity market gains were recorded in Viet Nam (4.4%) and Singapore (4.2%). Viet Nam's equity market was buoyed by an upward revision in the government's growth target for 2025 as well as new initiatives being implemented to gain emerging market status in the FTSE Russell Index. In Singapore, equity market growth was largely driven by positive investor sentiment over the Monetary Authority of Singapore's support measures for the stock market.[5] In contrast, Thailand's equity market posted the region's largest losses of –15.7% over its slow economic recovery: Its full-year 2024 GDP growth was among the weakest in the region. Risk premiums, captured by credit default swap (CDS) spreads, slightly narrowed in the region by a simple average of 1.9 bps during the review period, while declining 13.1 bps on a GDP-weighted basis, driven by the PRC. In December, all regional markets saw a rise in their respective CDS spreads on heightened uncertainty over the Federal Reserve's monetary stance and US economic policy (**Figure G**). The region's CDS spreads collectively narrowed in January on positive sentiment over the gradual implementation of US tariffs. In February, a few

Figure E: Foreign Capital Flows in Select Emerging East Asian Local Currency Bond Markets

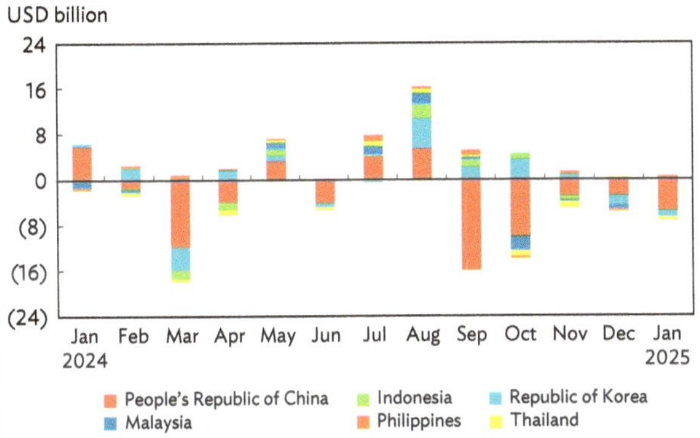

( ) = outflows, USD = United States dollar.

Notes:

1. The Republic of Korea and Thailand provided data on bond flows. For the People's Republic of China, Indonesia, Malaysia, and the Philippines, month-on-month changes in foreign holdings of local currency government bonds were used as a proxy for bond flows.
2. Data are as of 31 January 2025.
3. Figures were computed based on 31 January 2025 exchange rates and do not include currency effects.

Sources: People's Republic of China (Bloomberg LP); Indonesia (Directorate General of Budget Financing and Risk Management, Ministry of Finance); Republic of Korea (Financial Supervisory Service); Malaysia (Bank Negara Malaysia); Philippines (Bureau of the Treasury); and Thailand (Thai Bond Market Association).

Figure F: Changes in Equity Indexes in Select Emerging East Asian Markets

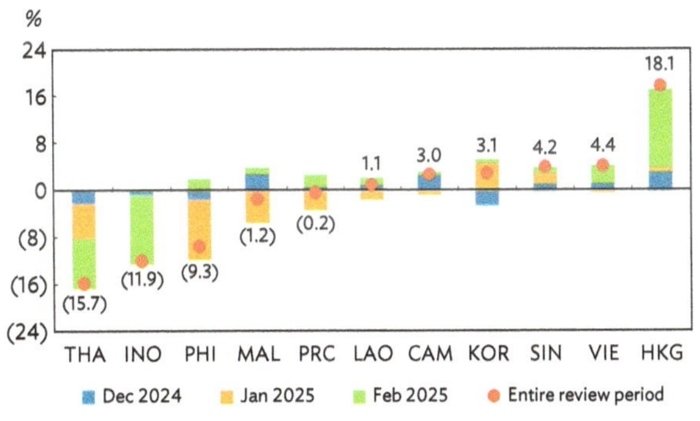

( ) = negative; CAM = Cambodia; PRC = People's Republic of China; HKG = Hong Kong, China; INO = Indonesia; KOR = Republic of Korea; LAO = Lao People's Democratic Republic; MAL = Malaysia; PHI = Philippines; SIN = Singapore; THA = Thailand; VIE = Viet Nam.

Note: The numbers above (below) each bar refer to the percentage change between 1 December 2024 and 28 February 2025.

Source: *AsianBondsOnline* calculations based on Bloomberg LP data.

[5] In February, the Monetary Authority of Singapore unveiled its intentions to implement the following measures, among others: (i) establish a SGD5 billion fund for investment placement with fund managers and tax exemptions for fund managers with substantial investment in Singapore-listed equities, (ii) limit the domestic portion investment requirement for foreign investors to exchange-listed assets, and (iii) offer a tax rebate for new listings and new secondary listings and a 5% concessionary tax rate on qualifying income for new fund managers listings.

Figure G: Changes in Credit Default Swap Spreads in Select Emerging East Asian Markets (senior 5-year)

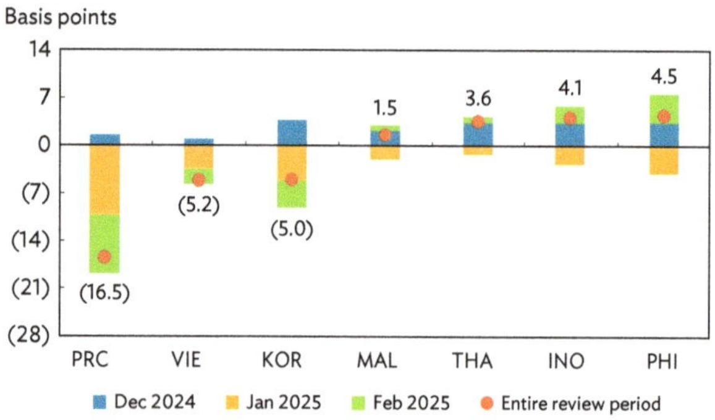

() = negative; PRC = People's Republic of China; INO = Indonesia; KOR = Republic of Korea; MAL = Malaysia; PHI = Philippines; THA = Thailand; VIE = Viet Nam.

Note: The numbers above (below) each bar refer to the change in spreads between 1 December 2024 and 28 February 2025.

Source: *AsianBondsOnline* calculations based on Bloomberg LP data.

markets witnessed continued risk premium narrowing. During the review period, risk premiums fell the most in the PRC (–16.5 bps) over expectations of continued support from the government.

Risks to the region's financial conditions outlook are tilted to the downside, primarily driven by the uncertainty surrounding policy shifts under the new US administration, particularly in trade. Uncertainty in US economic policies could affect the financial conditions outlook via negative investor sentiment as well as higher-for-longer interest rates in the US. As flagged by officials of the Federal Reserve and the ECB, changes in trade policies and associated rising tariffs could lead to higher costs, possibly disrupting disinflation patterns. Additionally, larger-than-expected shifts in US immigration (more restrictive) and fiscal (more expansionary) policies could also potentially hinder the disinflationary process. Persistent inflation could slow easing cycles in advanced economies. The US' prolonged higher interest rates presented challenges to regional financial stability during the review period via capital outflows. Delayed easing action in the US may affect regional central banks' easing cycles, slowing the decline in borrowing costs and weighing on growth. Within the region, uncertainty over stabilizing the property market and improving domestic economic performance in the PRC could also weaken investor sentiment in other regional markets. In the medium term, extreme weather events related to climate change could negatively impact growth and inflation. Meanwhile, sovereign sustainable bond issues help mobilize private sustainable bond finance to mitigate the impact of climate change, which is discussed in **Box 2**. A discussion on how sustainability-linked bonds can be made more effective in driving sustainable outcomes is presented in **Box 3**.

Box 1: Opportunities and Challenges of Artificial Intelligence for Financial Systems

The financial sector is data-intensive and among the most exposed to artificial intelligence (AI). The application of AI in finance is significantly changing how markets operate, risks are managed, and consumers interact with financial services.

The use of AI in finance is not something new. Traditional analytics have been applied in various functions throughout the financial system. For example, AI models have been used for rule-based risk analysis in financial intermediation, risk management and portfolio optimization in asset management, and fraud detection in payment systems. Machine learning methods have also been employed in various applications in the financial sector such as credit- and insurance-risk analysis, high-frequency trading, new liquidity management tools, and anti-money laundering (Aldasoro et al. 2024).

Generative AI (GenAI) is distinct from traditional analytics and machine learning methods in three aspects: automaticity, speed, and ubiquity (Shin 2024). GenAI has the ability to generate and execute transactions, even without human intervention. It enables the processing of huge amounts of data at a speed far beyond human capacity. Furthermore, it can be integrated across different activities and sectors of the economy.

GenAI offers vast opportunities for the financial sector across several functions including financial intermediation, insurance, asset management, and payment systems. Financial institutions have used GenAI to strengthen credit scoring, back-end processing, customer support, risk analysis, robo-advising, and know-your-customer processes. The **Table B1** below summarizes the opportunities to apply AI in finance.

While AI has created numerous benefits for the financial sector, there are some challenges related to its adoption. In particular, there are new risks associated with the use of GenAI. Since AI can be adopted across different functions, processes, and applications, financial systems will likely become more vulnerable to cybersecurity threats. Further, GenAI models are prone to the garbage-in-garbage-out problem, as they tend to capture and sustain biases and errors inherent in the underlying data that they have been trained on. The use of AI-generated strategies that rely on "black box" analysis suggests that it may be difficult to explain their predictions.[a] AI models could also generate "hallucinations," which are false or misleading information resulting from incorrect or insufficient training data and faulty assumptions. Furthermore, the use of GenAI can create systemic risks. Market concentration is rife across all layers of the AI supply chain—from hardware and

Table B1: Opportunities for Artificial Intelligence in the Financial Sector

	Financial Intermediation	Insurance	Asset Management	Payments
Traditional Analytics	Rule-based risk analysis, greater competition	Rule-based risk analysis, greater competition	Risk management, portfolio optimization, HF trading	Fraud detection
Machine Learning	Credit risk analysis, lower underwriting costs, financial inclusion	Insurance risk analysis, lower processing costs, fraud detection	Analysis of new data sources, HF trading	New liquidity management tools, fraud detection and AML
Generative AI	Enhanced credit scoring (unstructured data), easier back-end processing, better customer support	Better risk analysis with newly legible data, easier compliance	Robo-advising, asset embedding, new products, customer service	Enhanced KYC and AML processes

AI = artificial intelligence, AML = anti-money laundering, HF = high-frequency, KYC = know-your-customer.

Source: Adapted from Aldasoro et al. (2024).

This box was written by Leonardo Gambacorta (head of the Emerging Markets Unit) at the Bank for International Settlements and Gemma Estrada (senior economics officer) and Donghyun Park (economic advisor) of the Asian Development Bank. The views expressed here are those of the authors and not necessarily those of the Bank for International Settlements or the Asian Development Bank.

[a] "Black box" in AI refers to a system whose inputs and operations are not known to users. Black box AI models generate predictions and decisions without any clear explanation as to how they have been produced. Techtarget. Definition—What is Black Box AI?

continued on next page

Box 1 *continued*

cloud computing to training data and foundation models (Gambacorta and Shreeti 2025). Big tech players in the GenAI space are expanding their presence in the AI supply chain, integrating their services across different markets and reinforcing their dominance. AI supply chain concentration causes third-party dependencies (e.g., model, data, and algorithmic herding), resulting in more uniform behavior. This suggests that failures and disruptions within the AI systems of big tech players can have widespread effects that lead to overall financial instability.

A key challenge is to build AI regulations that recognize the risks and benefits of AI adoption. This would help maximize the benefits of AI for finance while minimizing its risks. The principles underlying AI regulations must encompass social and environmental well-being, transparency and accountability, and fairness and protection of privacy. Further, they must adhere to safety measures and human oversight, while being robust and reliable (Aldasoro et al. 2024). Different regulatory models for AI have been proposed. One model is a market-driven approach, in which the focus is on self-regulation and innovation. A second model is a state-driven approach, which focuses on political objectives and technology exports. A third model is rights-driven, in which the emphasis is on individual and social rights (Bradford 2023). The three models are not necessarily mutually exclusive and therefore can be adopted to varying degrees and combinations.

Given differences in economies' level of development and the extent of their AI adoption, global cooperation on AI regulation is critical. Economies stand to gain from harmonized regulatory standards and governance rules that enable the transfer of knowledge, uniform risk assessment, and the prevention of regulatory arbitrage.

To conclude, the adoption of AI can deliver potentially large benefits for the financial sector. However, AI also introduces significant risks such as market concentration, model hallucination, and cybersecurity risks. While AI can boost the productivity of the financial sector, it also poses systemic risks and potential market disruptions. To maximize the net benefits for finance, AI regulations must strike a balance between innovation and safety. Doing so requires international cooperation, transparency, and adaptable principles that can keep up with fast-evolving AI technologies.

References

I. Aldasoro, L. Gambacorta, A. Korinek, V. Shreeti, and M. Stein. 2024. Intelligent Financial System: How AI is Transforming Finance. *BIS Working Papers*. No. 1194. Bank for International Settlements (BIS).

A. Bradford. 2023. *Digital Empires: The Global Battle to Regulate Technology*. Oxford University Press.

L. Gambacorta and V. Shreeti. Forthcoming. The AI Supply Chain. *BIS Working Papers*. No. 154. BIS.

H.S. Shin. 2024. Artificial Intelligence and the Economy: Implications for Central Banks. *Annual Economic Report*, Chapter III. BIS.

Box 2: Sovereign Sustainable Bond Issuance and Sustainable Bond Market Development in Developing Asia

Sustainable bonds have become important instruments in directing capital toward eco-friendly and socially responsible investments. These debt instruments—issued by governments, corporations, and other entities—allocate funds to projects that meet certain environmental or social objectives. In developing Asia, sustainable bond markets have expanded rapidly during the past decade, driven by new investment opportunities, regulatory shifts and policy support, and rising investor demand (Giardino et al. 2024).[a]

In developing Asia, corporate issuers are the main players in the sustainable bond market. At the end of 2024, 70.5% of outstanding sustainable bonds in developing Asia were issued by corporates. However, this contrasts with the fact that government bonds accounted for 65.7% of total bonds outstanding in developing Asian markets at the end of 2024. Developing Asia's public sector share of sustainable bond issuance is less than in the world's largest sustainable bond market, the European Union, where 48.8% of sustainable bond outstanding at the end of 2024 were issued by governments.

Developing Asia can mobilize more private capital for sustainable investments through greater public sector participation. Ehlers et al. (2024) find that sovereign sustainable bond issuance can boost corporate sustainable bond issuance. Increased issuance can be facilitated by governments signaling their commitment to implementing renewable energy policy to fulfill net-zero pledges (Chesini 2024; Cheng, Ehlers, and Packer 2022; Capelle-Blancard et al. 2019), as well as through greater transparency via improved verification and reporting (Cheng, Ehlers, and Packer 2022; Jankovic, Vasic, and Kovacevic 2022). The study that this box is based on extends the findings of Ehlers et al. (2024) by examining the role of sovereign sustainable bond issuance on corporate sustainable bond market development in Asia. Specifically, we explore how the first sovereign issuance of sustainable bonds and ongoing buildup of sovereign sustainable bond issuances affect the size and diversification of corporate sustainable bond markets.

Our study follows Ehlers et al. (2024) and employs a panel regression approach with market-quarter fixed effects. The panel dataset encompasses nine developing Asian economies with sovereign sustainable bond issuances from the third quarter of 2014, when the first corporate sustainable bond was issued in developing Asia, to the second quarter of 2024, the most recent quarter for which data are available. The markets included in the sample are Hong Kong, China; Indonesia; India; the Republic of Korea; Malaysia; the Philippines; Singapore; Thailand; and Uzbekistan.

This study examines the impact of sovereign sustainable bond issuance on several corporate sustainable bond market development indicators, including size, which is captured by the proportion of sustainable corporate bond issuances as a share of total corporate bond issuances during the quarter (size); the proportion of local currency sustainable bond issuance to total sustainable bond issuance during the quarter (LCY); the natural logarithm of the number of first-time corporate sustainable bond issuance (first time), as well as the number of unique corporate sustainable bond issuers during the quarter (unique); and the Herfindahl–Hirschman Index of cumulative corporate sustainable bond issuance from the first issuance until the current quarter by sector (HHI-sector) and by issuer (HHI-issuer) to measure market concentration.

To capture sovereign sustainable bond issuance, this study includes several measures. The first is a binary variable (sovereign debut) that denotes the quarter of the first sovereign issuance of sustainable bonds in a market. The second measure is the proportion of a market's cumulative sovereign sustainable issuance to cumulative total sovereign bond issuance by quarter (sustainable share of sovereign issuances) to reflect the efforts of government spending on sustainable activities. To gauge whether the currency denomination of a sovereign sustainable bond issuance affects its impacts, this study also includes a binary variable to indicate the first LCY sovereign sustainable bond issuance (LCY sovereign debut).

The analysis controls for sustainable bond market development using total sustainable bonds outstanding (total bonds outstanding) during the quarter, overall market financing conditions (total bond issuance) during the quarter, and domestic bond market development (outstanding bonds as a share of gross domestic product) during the quarter.

This box was written by Resi Ong Olivares (consultant) and Shu Tian (principal economist) of the Asian Development Bank.

[a] Developing Asia comprises the 46 developing member economies of the Asian Development Bank.

continued on next page

Box 2 *continued*

The empirical results are reported in **Figure B2**. As shown in **panel A**, there is a significant and positive association between sovereign debuts and corporate sustainable bond market development. Sovereign debuts are related to a 4.0% increase in overall corporate bond issuance and a substantial 26.2% increase in LCY corporate bond issuance. Furthermore, sovereign debt is significantly associated with declines of 15.8% and 35.6%, respectively, in market concentration in terms of both sustainable bond sectors and issuers. Issuing LCY sovereign sustainable bonds is also beneficial to market development. An LCY sovereign sustainable bond debut is related to a 20.9% increase in LCY corporate bond issuance (**panel B**); a 40.9% increase in unique issuers; and declines of 14.1% and 25.0% in market concentration as measured by sectors and issuers, respectively. These results indicate that sovereign sustainable bonds are related to corporate sustainable bond market development. As shown in **panel C** of Figure B2, a 1% higher share of sovereign sustainable bond issuance is related to a 0.05% increase in the volume of total corporate sustainable bonds outstanding, 0.69% more LCY corporate sustainable bond issuance, and 0.69% more unique corporate sustainable bond issuers.

These findings provide evidence that sovereign issuances of sustainable bonds can help catalyze private sustainable finance in developing Asia. As discussed in Ehlers et al. (2024), sovereign sustainable bond issuance can promote corporate sustainable bond issuance via signaling and transparency in reporting. In developing Asia, we find that sovereign issuance can increase the number of corporate sustainable bond issuers and broaden corporate sustainable market participation, thereby reducing market concentration. These findings have significant implications for policymakers aiming to accelerate the transition to a more sustainable economy. By strategically issuing sovereign sustainable bonds, governments can raise capital for sustainable projects and catalyze private sector engagement in sustainable finance. The findings of this study will guide future exploration of possible working channels in developing Asia and the long-term impact of sovereign issuance on issuer performance and broader economic outcomes.

Figure B2: Impacts of Sovereign Sustainable Bond Issuance on Corporate Sustainable Bond Issuance

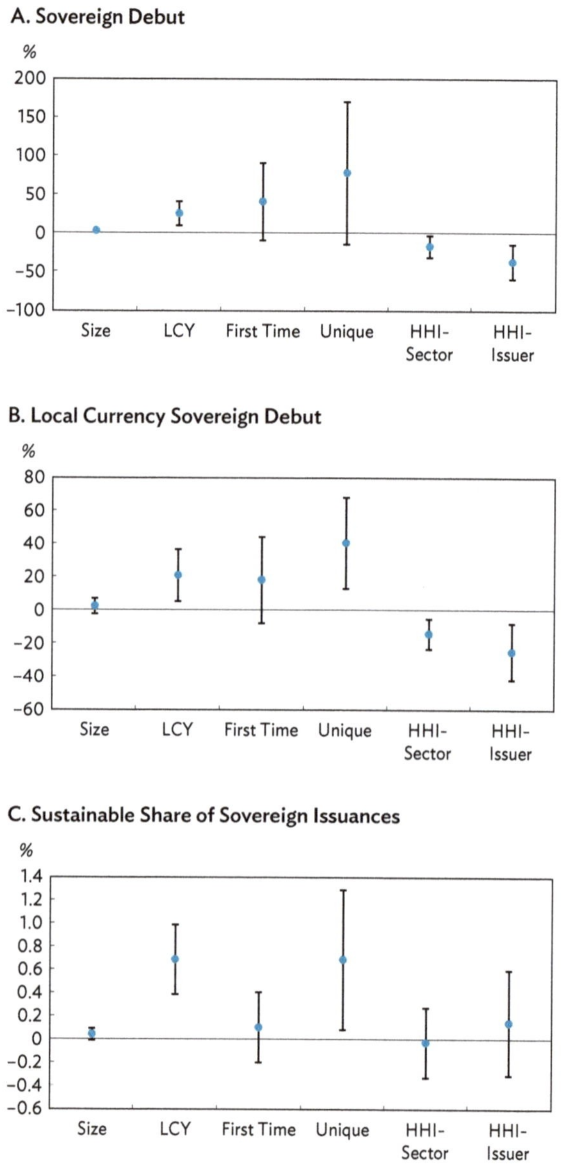

HHI = Herfindahl–Hirschman Index, LCY = local currency.
Source: Authors' calculations.

continued on next page

Box 2 *continued*

References

G. Capelle-Blancard, P. Crifo, M.A. Diaye, R. Oueghlissi, and B. Scholtens. 2019. Sovereign Bond Yield Spreads and Sustainability: An Empirical Analysis of OECD Countries. *Journal of Banking & Finance*. 98. pp. 156–69.

G. Cheng, T. Ehlers, and F. Packer. 2022. Sovereigns and Sustainable Bonds: Challenges and New Options. *BIS Quarterly Review*. 47 (September). pp. 1–10.

G. Chesini. 2024. Can Sovereign Green Bonds Accelerate the Transition to Net-Zero Greenhouse Gas Emissions? *International Advances in Economic Research*. 30 (4). pp. 1–21.

R. Dittmar, and K. Yuan. 2008. Do Sovereign Bonds Benefit Corporate Bonds in Emerging Markets? *The Review of Financial Studies*. 21 (5). 1983–2014.

T. Ehlers, F. Packer, G. Cheng, and Y. Xiao. 2024. Sovereign Green Bonds: A Catalyst for Sustainable Debt Market Development? SSRN No. 4874999.

A. Giardino, M. Pelli, D.A. Raitzer, F. Bosello, L. Campagnolo, and G. Mansi. 2024. *Asia-Pacific Climate Report 2024*. Manila: Asian Development Bank.

I. Jankovic, V. Vasic, and V. Kovacevic. 2022. Does Transparency Matter? Evidence from Panel Analysis of the EU Government Green Bonds. *Energy Economics*. 114. 106325.

R. Olivares, S. Tian, and B. Zhao. 2024. Sovereign Sustainable Bond Issuance and Sustainable Bond Market Development in Developing Asia. *ADB Working Paper Series*. Manila.

K. Yuan. 2005. The Liquidity Service of Benchmark Securities. Journal of the European Economic Association. 3 (5): 1156–80.

Box 3: Strengthening Sustainability-Linked Bonds

Sustainability-linked bonds (SLBs) are an innovative debt instrument designed to embed financial incentives that encourage issuers to meet predetermined sustainability targets. By linking financial performance to sustainability outcomes, SLBs aim to enhance issuer accountability and mitigate concerns about greenwashing in the sustainable debt market. The overwhelming majority of SLBs have a coupon step-up penalty as the embedded financial incentive, which is a rise in the interest cost if the issuer fails to meet preset sustainability targets by a predetermined deadline (i.e., target date).

However, for SLBs to be truly effective, the embedded financial incentives must be significant enough to influence issuer behavior. Evidence suggests that this is often not the case: The average coupon step-up penalty accounts for less than 12% of the coupon rate.

Figure B3: Callability of Corporate Bonds by Bond Type

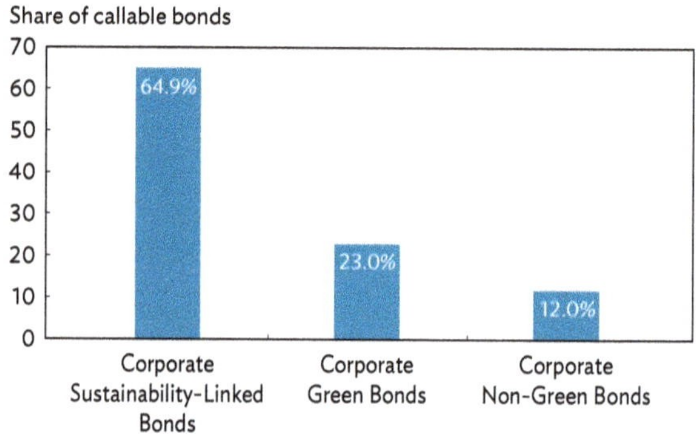

Sources: Ul Haq and Doumbia (2022) for sustainability-linked bonds and green bonds; Dias (2021) for non-green bonds.

Ul Haq and Doumbia (2022) highlights certain bond features that weaken SLBs' financial incentives regardless of the penalty size. Their study sheds light on two specific features that may dilute the effectiveness of SLBs in promoting sustainable impacts: (i) the timing of penalties and (ii) the ability for early redemption of a bond by the issuer.

First, many SLBs set sustainability target dates near the end of the bond's tenor, meaning financial penalties for noncompliance apply to only a few remaining coupon payments. This significantly reduces the financial consequences for issuers that fail to meet their targets. The problem is further compounded by the fact that SLBs with higher step-up penalties tend to have later target dates, effectively diluting even large penalties. To improve accountability, SLBs should incorporate multiple interim targets throughout the bond's life, ensuring that financial incentives remain in place over time and that issuers face ongoing accountability.

Second, call options embedded in SLBs also allow issuers to minimize or avoid penalties. Many issuers retain the option to redeem their bonds before or close to sustainability target dates, effectively allowing them to sidestep penalties if sustainability targets are not met. SLBs are five times more likely to be callable than conventional corporate bonds, and most callable SLBs impose no additional financial penalty for early redemption even if sustainability targets are unmet, further undermining the credibility of financial incentives (**Figure B3**). Strengthening SLB structures by applying penalties if bonds are called early can help prevent issuers from exploiting this loophole.

Addressing these structural weaknesses—by setting multiple or timely target dates and ensuring adequate penalties on early redemption—can make SLBs a more credible tool for driving sustainability outcomes. This is especially critical for high-emission issuers, who are more likely to take advantage of these loopholes. Industry standards should incorporate these best practices, while regulators can enhance transparency by requiring disclosure of these structural features. External reviewers can also expand their scope to cover the materiality of financial incentives in addition to that of sustainability targets. Strengthening SLBs in this manner will help ensure that they fulfill their intended role of mobilizing capital for sustainability while delivering real impacts.

References

B.M. Dias. 2021. The Relationship Between Corporate Green Bond Yields and Firm Leverage. *Catolica Lisbon Business & Economics Working Paper*. https://repositorio.ucp.pt/handle/10400.14/34137.

I. Ul Haq and D. Doumbia. 2022. Structural Loopholes in Sustainability-Linked Bonds. *World Bank Policy Research Working Paper*. No. 10200. World Bank.

This box was written by Imtiaz Ul Haq (economist) of the Economics and Market Research Team at the International Finance Corporation, which is a part of the World Bank Group.

Bond Market Developments in the Fourth Quarter of 2024

Section 1. Local Currency Bonds Outstanding

The emerging East Asian local currency (LCY) bond market grew at a faster annual rate in 2024 than bond markets in advanced economies, although the amount of LCY bonds outstanding as a share of regional gross domestic product (GDP) remained low at the end of December.[6] The size of the LCY bond market in emerging East Asia reached USD26.3 trillion at the end of 2024, increasing 9.6% year-on-year (y-o-y) and surpassing the growth of 5.0% y-o-y in the United States' (US) bond market (USD39.7 trillion) and 5.1% y-o-y in the European Union 20's (EU-20) bond market (equivalent to USD21.0 trillion) (**Figure 1A**). In Q4 2024, regional LCY bonds outstanding grew

Figure 1: Local Currency Bonds Outstanding and Issuance

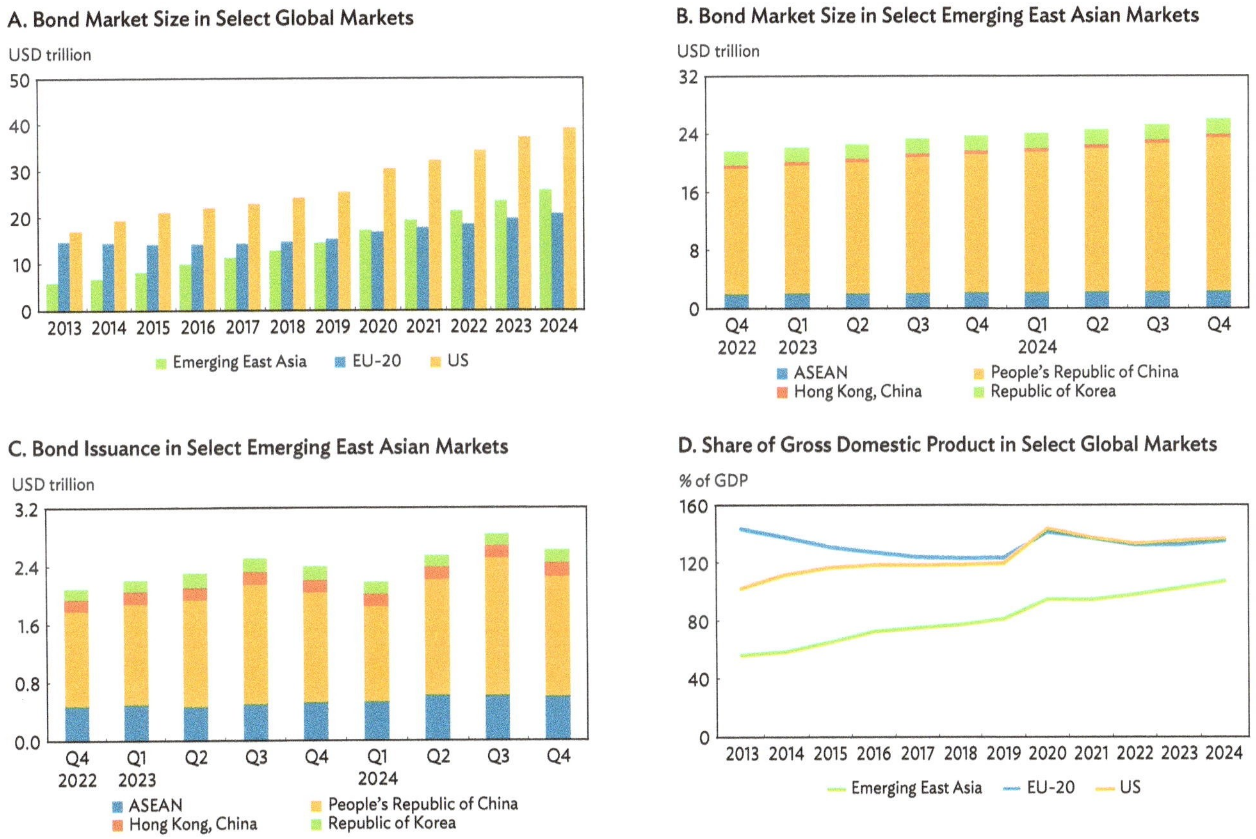

ASEAN = Association of Southeast Asian Nations, EU- 20 = European Union 20, GDP = gross domestic product, Q1 = first quarter, Q2 = second quarter, Q3 = third quarter, Q4 = fourth quarter, US = United States, USD = United States dollar.

Notes:

1. ASEAN comprises the markets of Indonesia, Malaysia, the Philippines, Singapore, Thailand, and Viet Nam.
2. Emerging East Asia is defined to include the Association of Southeast Asian Nations plus the People's Republic of China; Hong Kong, China; and the Republic of Korea.
3. The EU-20 includes the member markets of Austria, Belgium, Croatia, Cyprus, Estonia, Finland, France, Germany, Greece, Ireland, Italy, Latvia, Lithuania, Luxembourg, Malta, the Netherlands, Portugal, Slovakia, Slovenia, and Spain.

Source: *AsianBondsOnline* calculations based on various local market sources.

[6] Emerging East Asia is defined to include member states of the Association of Southeast Asian Nations plus the People's Republic of China; Hong Kong, China; and the Republic of Korea.

3.1% quarter-on-quarter (q-o-q), up from 2.7% q-o-q in the previous quarter, partly due to a lower volume of maturities in both government and corporate bonds (**Figure 1B**). This rapid expansion in Q4 2024 was primarily supported by continued issuance of government bonds in the People's Republic of China (PRC), which were aimed at supporting the slowing economy. Increased public and private sector issuance in Hong Kong, China; the Republic of Korea; and Singapore also contributed to growth in the region's overall LCY bond stock during the quarter (**Figure 1C**). However, relative to GDP, the emerging East Asian LCY bond market still lags behind those of the EU-20 and the US (**Figure 1D**). At the end of 2024, the region's LCY bond market was equivalent to 108.0% of emerging East Asia's GDP, compared to 136.0% in the EU-20 and 137.7% in the US. Nonetheless, the emerging East Asian LCY bond market's size relative to regional GDP has nearly doubled since 2013.

The regional LCY bond stock expanded in 2024, largely driven by strong growth in Viet Nam, Indonesia, and the PRC. Viet Nam, the smallest LCY bond market in the region, posted emerging East Asia's fastest annual growth in 2024 at 18.9% y-o-y, supported by robust expansion in both the government and corporate bond segments (**Figure 2A**). Indonesia was next with 16.7% y-o-y growth, supported by growth in government and corporate bonds amid lower borrowing costs. Following was the PRC with 10.5% y-o-y growth as its LCY bond market reached a size of

Figure 2: Local Currency Bonds Outstanding in Select Emerging East Asian Markets

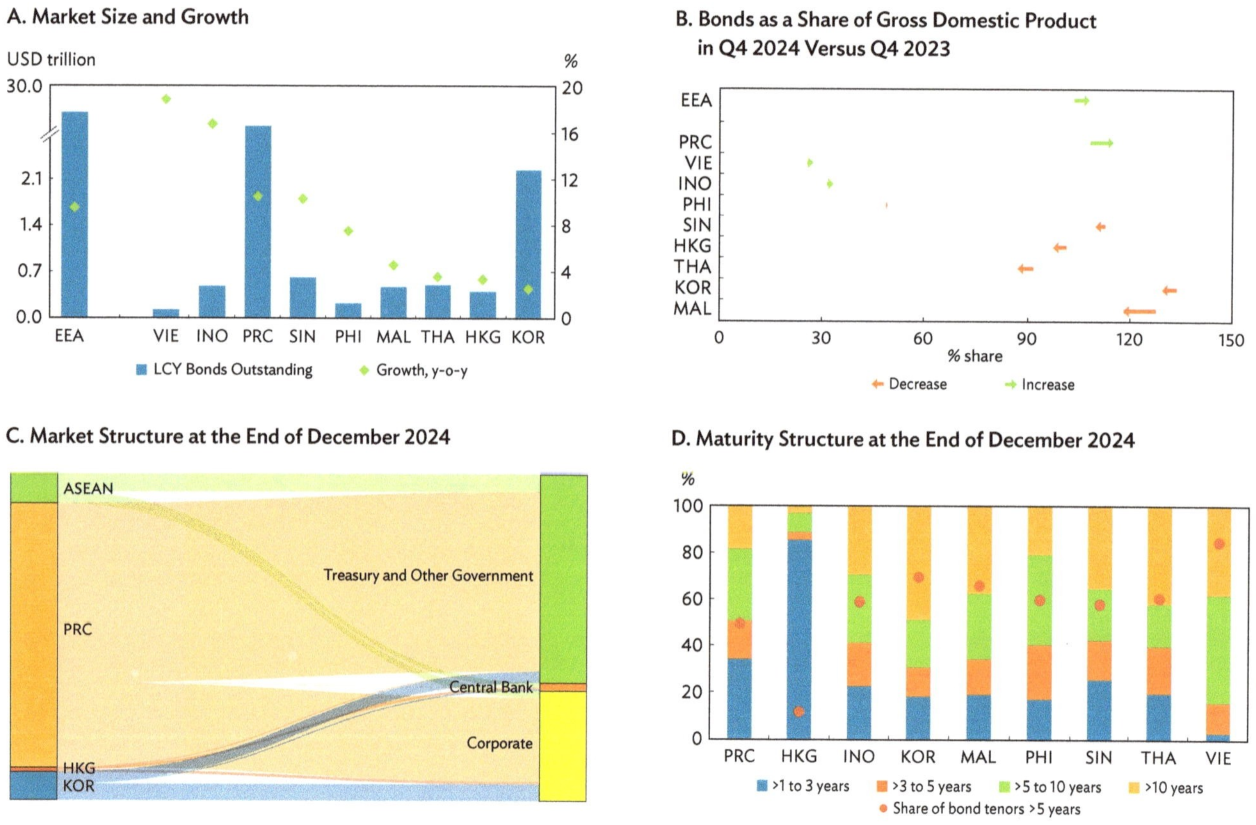

ASEAN = Association of Southeast Asian Nations; PRC = People's Republic of China; EEA = emerging East Asia; HKG = Hong Kong, China; INO = Indonesia; KOR = Republic of Korea; LCY = local currency; MAL = Malaysia; PHI = Philippines; Q4 = fourth quarter; SIN = Singapore; THA = Thailand; USD = United States dollar; VIE = Viet Nam; y-o-y = year-on-year.

Notes:

1. Emerging East Asia is defined to include the Association of Southeast Asian Nations plus the People's Republic of China; Hong Kong, China; and the Republic of Korea.
2. Growth rates are calculated from a local currency base and do not include currency effects. For emerging East Asia, growth figures are based on 31 December 2024 currency exchange rates and do not include currency effects.
3. GDP data are from CEIC Company.

Source: *AsianBondsOnline* calculations based on various local market sources.

USD21.3 trillion at the end of 2024, maintaining an 80.8% share of the regional total. These three markets were also the only ones in emerging East Asia in 2024 to increase their percentage of LCY bonds relative to GDP compared to a year earlier, contributing to the LCY bond market's higher overall share of GDP in the region (**Figure 2B**). The PRC remained the largest bond market in emerging East Asia, while the aggregate bond stock of members of the Association of Southeast Asian Nations (ASEAN) expanded to USD2.4 trillion at the end of December, representing a 9.2% share of the regional total. Treasury bonds represented 63.8% of the region's total LCY bonds outstanding at the end of December, while corporate bonds and central bank securities accounted for the remaining 33.8% and 2.5% shares, respectively (**Figure 2C**). At the end of 2024, 54.0% of outstanding Treasury bonds in the region had remaining maturities of over 5 years (**Figure 2D**). The size-weighted average tenor of outstanding Treasury bonds in emerging East Asia was 9.2 years at the end of 2024.

Institutional investors continued to account for substantial holdings of the region's Treasury bonds in Q4 2024. At the end of December, the bond holdings of banks averaged 34.7% across all markets in the region, followed by insurance and pension funds at 28.9%, while all other investor groups accounted for average shares of 17.2% or less. In the PRC, banks were the dominant holders of bonds at the end of December with a 66.6% share, although this was down from its roughly 70.0% share in the first half of 2024 due to the People's Bank of China's measures to limit speculative trading in government bonds (**Figure 3**). Meanwhile, the relative share of insurance and pension funds' bond holdings was the largest in the region in Viet Nam at 59.4%. Indonesia is the only regional market where the central bank was the largest investor group at the end of 2024, with a share of 26.8%, as Bank Indonesia continued to purchase Treasury bonds as part of its monetary operations to support the domestic currency and the government bond market. Bank Indonesia committed to purchase about IDR150 trillion worth of bonds in the secondary market in 2025. Within the region, the PRC and Viet Nam had the least diversified investor profiles, as reflected by their high Herfindahl–Hirschman Index scores, while Indonesia and the Republic of Korea had the most diversified ownership structure in the region.[7]

Figure 3: Investor Profiles of Local Currency Treasury Bonds in Select Emerging East Asian Markets

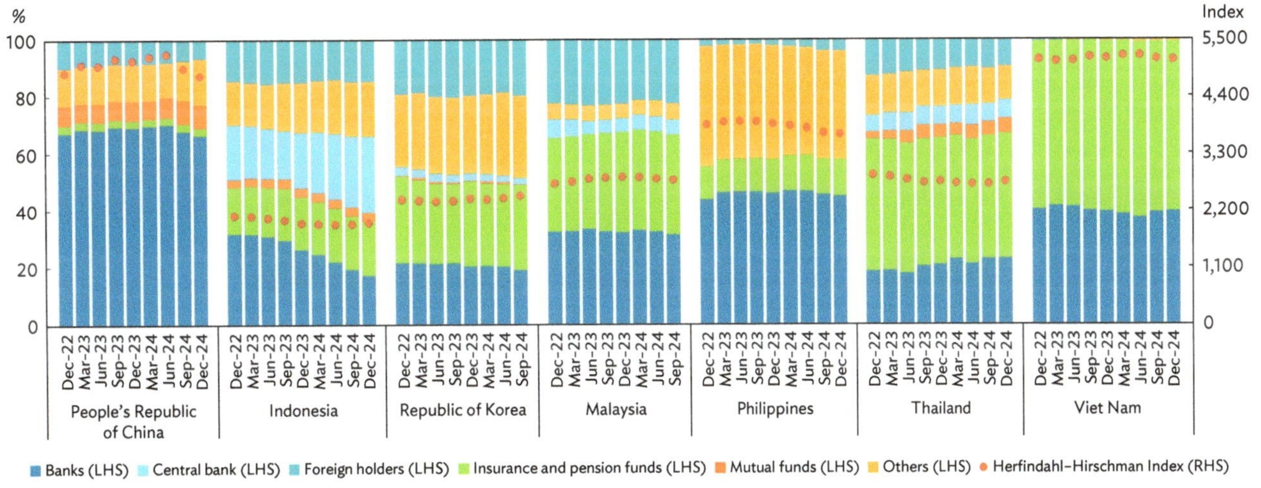

LHS = left-hand side, RHS = right-hand side.

Notes:
1. Data for the Republic of Korea and Malaysia are up to September 2024.
2. "Others" include government institutions, individuals, securities companies, custodians, private corporations, and all other investors not elsewhere classified.
3. The Herfindahl–Hirschman Index is a commonly accepted measure of market concentration. In this case, the index was used to measure the investor profile diversification of the local currency bond markets and is calculated by summing the squared share of each investor group in the bond market.

Sources: People's Republic of China (CEIC Data Company); Indonesia (Directorate General of Budget Financing and Risk Management, Ministry of Finance); Republic of Korea (Bank of Korea); Malaysia (Bank Negara Malaysia); Philippines (Bureau of the Treasury); Thailand (Bank of Thailand); and Viet Nam (Ministry of Finance).

[7] The Herfindahl–Hirschman Index is a commonly accepted measure of market concentration. The index is used to measure the investor profile diversification of the region's local currency bond markets and is calculated by summing the squared share of each investor group in the bond market.

Section 2. Local Currency Bond Issuance

LCY bond issuance contracted in emerging East Asia in Q4 2024. Total LCY bond issuance declined 7.5% q-o-q to USD2.6 trillion in Q4 2024, a reversal from the 11.4% q-o-q growth in the third quarter (Q3) 2024, as both the government and corporate bond segments posted declines (**Figure 4A**). Despite the contraction in Q4 2024, the region's annual issuance rose to USD10.2 billion in 2024 from USD9.5 billion in 2023. Issuance of government bonds fell 16.3% q-o-q in Q4 2024 as most governments had already fulfilled their borrowing requirements in the previous 3 quarters of the year. Issuance of corporate bonds marginally fell 1.2% q-o-q in Q4 2024 as the contraction in the PRC (7.3% q-o-q), which comprised 76.1% of the region's corporate issuance total during the quarter, offset the increases in Hong Kong, China; the Republic of Korea; and some ASEAN markets (**Figure 4B**). However, the largest corporate bond issuances in the region in Q4 2024 still came from the PRC as major banks continued to raise capital to comply with regulatory requirements. These included the CNY40.0 billion (USD5.5 billion) 10-year bond issued by the Industrial and Commercial Bank of China and the perpetual bonds in the same amount issued by the Agricultural Bank of China. Other notable corporate issuances in the region during Q4 2024 included the HKD8.0 billion 5-year bond from the Hong Kong Mortgage Corporation and Thailand's Siam Cement's THB30.0 billion (USD0.9 billion) 4-year bond.

Figure 4: Local Currency Bond Issuance in Select Emerging East Asian Markets

A. Percentage Contribution to Growth by Bond Type

B. Market Structure in the Fourth Quarter of 2024

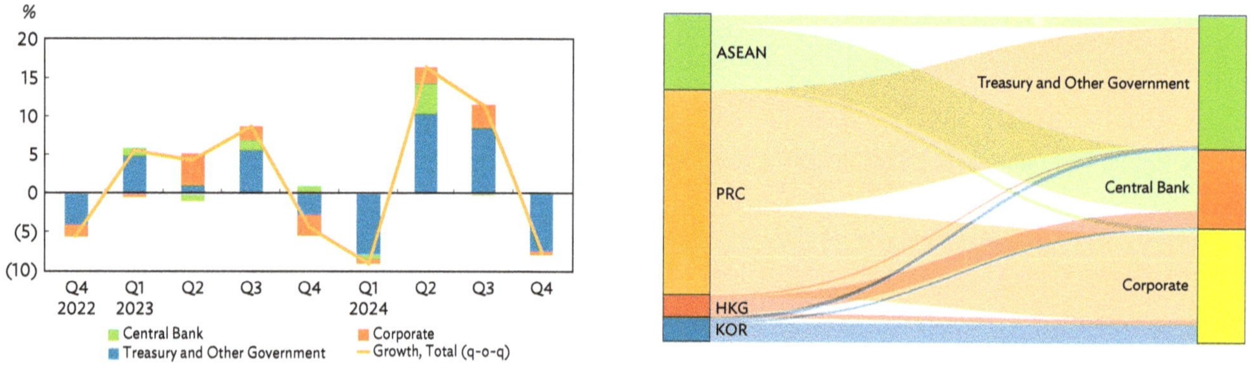

() = negative; ASEAN = Association of Southeast Asian Nations; PRC = People's Republic of China; HKG = Hong Kong, China; KOR = Republic of Korea; Q1 = first quarter; Q2 = second quarter; Q3 = third quarter; Q4 = fourth quarter; q-o-q = quarter-on-quarter.

Notes:
1. ASEAN comprises the markets of Indonesia, Malaysia, the Philippines, Singapore, Thailand, and Viet Nam.
2. Figures were computed based on 31 December 2024 currency exchange rates and do not include currency effects.

Source: *AsianBondsOnline* calculations based on various local market sources.

A majority of Treasury bond issuance in Q4 2024 continued to carry medium- and long-term tenors. Bonds with tenors of more than 5 years comprised 53.9% of total issuance in the region in Q4 2024; this share was even higher for ASEAN markets at 71.8% (**Figure 5A**). In particular, bonds issued with tenors of more than 5 years as a share of total issuance during the quarter was highest in Singapore (100%), Viet Nam (82.8%), and Thailand (71.8%) (**Figure 5B**). The corresponding share was lowest in Hong Kong, China (0.6%) as nearly all of its Q4 2024 issuance had tenors of less than 3 years. These bonds were mostly issued for the purpose of providing benchmark rates, improving market liquidity, and strengthening bond market development.

Figure 5: Maturity Structure of Local Currency Treasury Bond Issuance in Select Emerging East Asian Markets

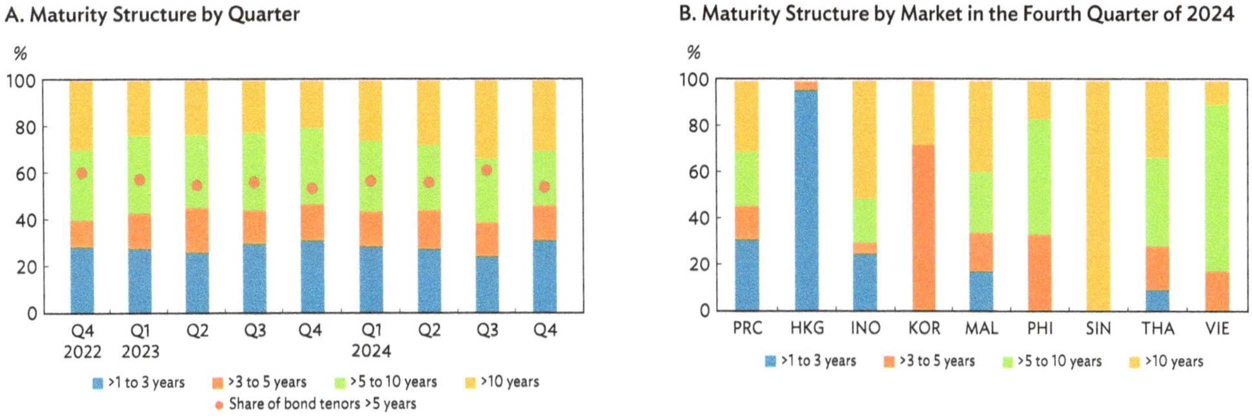

PRC = People's Republic of China; HKG = Hong Kong, China; INO = Indonesia; KOR = Republic of Korea; MAL = Malaysia; PHI = Philippines; Q1 = first quarter; Q2 = second quarter; Q3 = third quarter; Q4 = fourth quarter; SIN = Singapore; THA = Thailand; VIE = Viet Nam.

Notes:
1. Figures were computed based on 31 December 2024 currency exchange rates and do not include currency effects.
2. Treasury bonds are local-currency-denominated, fixed-income securities issued by a government with maturities longer than 1 year.

Source: *AsianBondsOnline* calculations based on various local market sources.

The average size-weighted tenor of Treasury bond issuance shortened in Q4 2024. The average size-weighted tenor of Treasury bond issuances in emerging East Asia decreased to 7.3 years in Q4 2024 from 10.0 years in Q3 2024 (**Figure 6A**). This was driven by non-ASEAN markets where the average length fell to 6.7 years in Q4 2024 from 10.0 years in the previous quarter. Meanwhile, the average size-weighted tenor of Treasury bond issuance in ASEAN markets slightly rose to 11.5 years from 10.3 years during the same period. Among Non-ASEAN markets, the Republic of Korea declined the most as the government issued only medium-term bonds during the quarter compared to long-term bonds (from 20 years to 50 years) in Q3 2024. In ASEAN markets, Singapore had the longest average tenor for Treasury bond issuance in Q4 2024 due to its issuance of SGD1.5 billion worth of 50-year Green Infrastructure Singapore Savings Bonds in October. Thailand and Viet Nam followed with size-weighted average issuance tenors of 12.7 years and 11.0 years, respectively (**Figure 6B**).

Figure 6: Average Size-Weighted Tenor of Treasury Bond Issuance in Select Emerging East Asian Markets

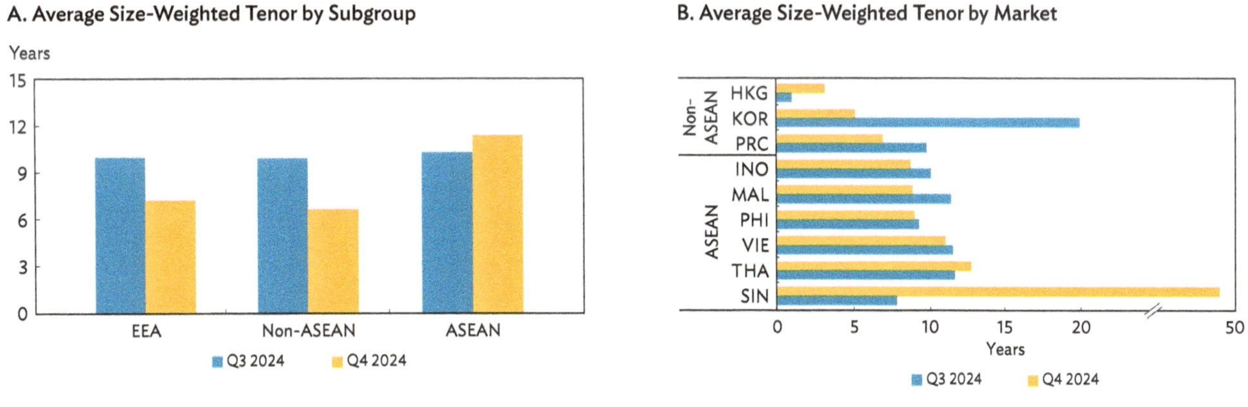

ASEAN = Association of Southeast Asian Nations; PRC = People's Republic of China; EEA = emerging East Asia; HKG = Hong Kong, China; INO = Indonesia; KOR = Republic of Korea; MAL = Malaysia; PHI = Philippines; Q3 = third quarter; Q4 = fourth quarter; SIN = Singapore; THA = Thailand; VIE = Viet Nam.

Notes:
1. Figures were computed based on 31 December 2024 currency exchange rates and do not include currency effects.
2. Treasury bonds are local-currency-denominated, fixed-income securities issued by a government with maturities longer than 1 year.

Source: *AsianBondsOnline* calculations based on various local market sources.

Section 3: Intra-Regional Bond Issuance

Intra-regional bond issuance in emerging East Asia bounced back in Q4 2024.[8] Intra-regional bond issuance in emerging East Asia reached USD11.1 billion in Q4 2024 on growth of 5.2% q-o-q, reversing the 5.8% q-o-q contraction in Q3 2024. Growth was mainly driven by increased debt sales in Singapore, the Republic of Korea, and Malaysia (**Figure 7A**). Meanwhile, Hong Kong, China recorded a minimal decline of 1.7% q-o-q in issuance as the government and corporates preferred issuing LCY-denominated bonds amid improved domestic economic conditions. Despite the decline, Hong Kong, China remained the region's top issuer, accounting for 83.5% of the total. Hong Kong, China saw notable issuances related to sustainable bonds during the quarter, including CNY-denominated green bonds worth CNY2.2 billion from CCCI Treasure and carbon-neutrality bond worth CNY1.0 billion from China Power International Development. The financial sector and CNY-denominated bonds dominated emerging East Asia's intra-regional bond issuance in Q4 2024 (**Figure 7B**). For full-year 2024, total intra-regional debt sales in the region reached USD41.6 billion, reflecting an annual decline of 11.3% from USD46.9 billion in 2023. Intra-regional bond issuance in the region predominantly featured short-term tenors in Q4 2024. Bonds with maturities of 5 years or less accounted for 87.9% of the intra-regional issuance total during the quarter (**Figure 7C**). Consequently, the size-weighted average maturity of issued intra-regional bonds in Q4 2024 was 2.6 years.

Figure 7: Intra-Regional Bond Issuance in Select Emerging East Asian Markets

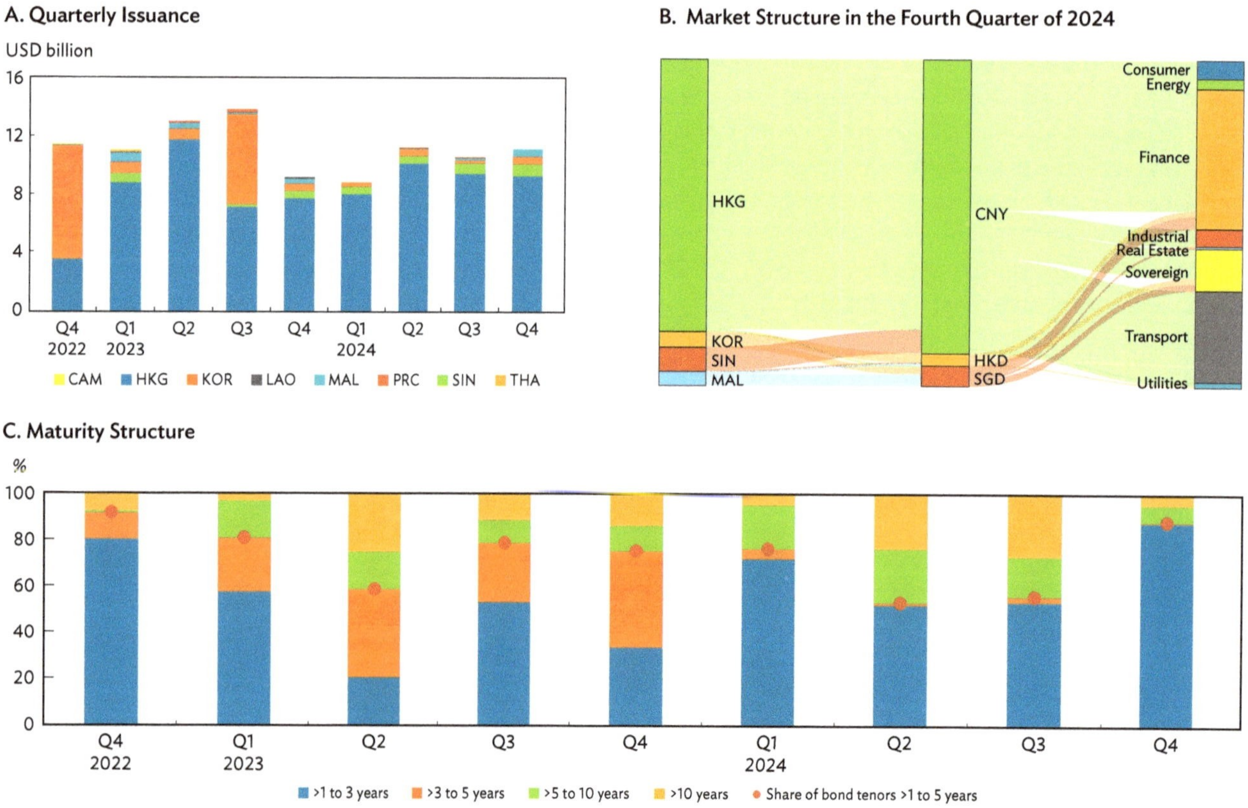

CAM = Cambodia; PRC = People's Republic of China; CNY = Chinese yuan; HKD = Hong Kong dollar; HKG = Hong Kong, China; KOR = Republic of Korea; LAO = Lao People's Democratic Republic; MAL = Malaysia; Q1 = first quarter; Q2 = second quarter; Q3 = third quarter; Q4 = fourth quarter; SGD = Singapore dollar; SIN = Singapore; THA = Thailand; USD = United States dollar.

Notes:

1. Emerging East Asia is defined to include member states of the Association of Southeast Asian Nations plus the People's Republic of China; Hong Kong, China; and the Republic of Korea.
2. Intra-regional bond issuance is defined as emerging East Asian bond issuance denominated in a regional currency excluding the issuer's home currency.
3. Figures were computed based on 31 December 2024 currency exchange rates and do not include currency effects.

Source: *AsianBondsOnline* calculations based on Bloomberg LP data.

[8] Intra-regional bond issuance is defined as emerging East Asian bond issuance denominated in a regional currency excluding the issuer's home currency.

Section 4. G3 Currency Bond Issuance

Emerging East Asian G3 currency bond issuance declined in Q4 2024 from the previous quarter.[9] G3 currency bond issuance in the region slowed to USD60.9 billion in Q4 2024, down 14.9% q-o-q, largely driven by reduced government issuance as they had mostly fulfilled their respective foreign currency borrowing plans in the earlier quarters of the year (**Figure 8A**). The governments of the Republic of Korea, the Philippines, and the Hong Kong Special Administrative Region of the PRC had no issuance in Q4 2024 after having issued in past quarters. Meanwhile, Indonesia still saw some sovereign G3 bond issuance in Q4 2024, albeit lower than in Q3 2024, as part of its front-loading plan for the 2025 budget. The PRC led all regional G3 bond issuance, accounting for 55.4% of the total in Q4 2024 on growth of 13.8% q-o-q that was buoyed by a return of the government to the offshore bond market after a 3-year hiatus (**Figure 8B**). Despite a 25.5% q-o-q contraction, ASEAN economies' G3 bond issuance of USD16.1 billion accounted for a 26.4% regional share. Within emerging East Asia, Bank Indonesia remained the top issuer of G3 currency bonds in Q4 2024 as it continued to issue USD-denominated securities as part of its monetary operations. The next largest issuer was the Government of the PRC as it issued USD- and EUR-denominated bonds during the quarter. For full-year 2024, G3 bond issuance in emerging East Asia totaled USD245.3 billion, up 31.5% from USD186.5 billion in 2023 amid moderating interest rates.

Figure 8: G3 Currency Bond Issuance in Select Emerging East Asian Markets

A. Monthly Bond Issuance | **B. Market Share in the Fourth Quarter of 2024**

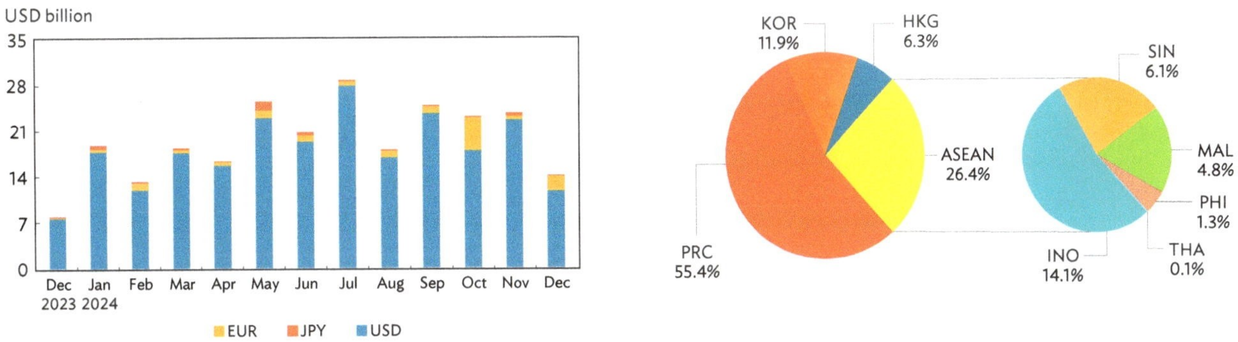

ASEAN = Association of Southeast Asian Nations; PRC = People's Republic of China; EUR = euro; HKG = Hong Kong, China; INO = Indonesia; JPY = Japanese yen; KOR = Republic of Korea; MAL = Malaysia; PHI = Philippines; SIN = Singapore; THA = Thailand; USD = United States dollar.

Notes:

1. Emerging East Asia is defined to include member states of the Association of Southeast Asian Nations plus the People's Republic of China; Hong Kong, China; and the Republic of Korea.
2. G3 currency bonds are denominated in either euros, Japanese yen, or United States dollars.
3. Figures were computed based on 31 December 2024 currency exchange rates and do not include currency effects.

Source: *AsianBondsOnline* calculations based on Bloomberg LP data.

[9] G3 currency bonds are bonds denominated in either euros, Japanese yen, or United States dollars.

Section 5. Yield Curve Movements

Most markets in emerging East Asia saw a widening of the 10-year and 2-year yield spread between 1 December 2024 and 28 February 2025. Six out of the nine markets in the region saw a rise in their respective 10-year and 2-year yield spread on the less dovish stance of the US Federal Reserve and uncertainty regarding the path of US economic policy (**Figure 9A and 9B**). On the other hand, both the Republic of Korea and Thailand saw a narrowing of yield spreads as their respective central banks eased monetary policy during the review period amid growth concerns. In the PRC, the yield spread declined as the government pledged in December to keep monetary policy "moderately loose," though the People's Bank of China did not ease in January or February.

Figure 9: Yield Spread Between 10-Year and 2-Year Local Currency Government Bonds in Select Emerging East Asian Markets

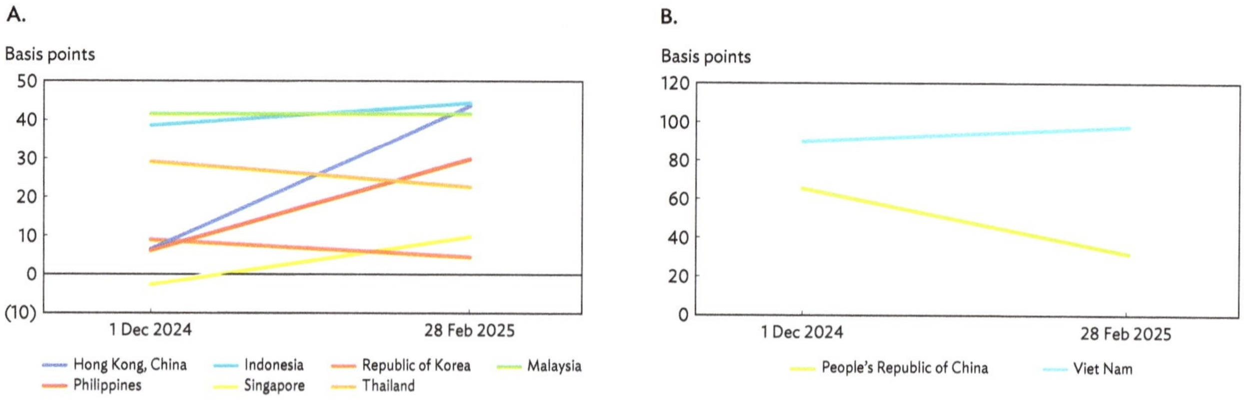

( ) = negative.

Sources: *AsianBondsOnline* calculations based on Bloomberg LP and Thai Bond Market Association data.

Appendix

Table A1: Size and Composition of Select Emerging East Asian Local Currency Bond Markets

	Q4 2023		Q3 2024		Q4 2024			Growth Rate (%)	
								Q4 2024	
	Amount (USD billion)	% of GDP	Amount (USD billion)	% of GDP	Amount (USD billion)	% share	% of GDP	q-o-q	y-o-y
People's Republic of China									
Total	19,769	108.4	21,326	112.3	21,252	100.0	115.0	3.6	10.5
Treasury and Other Government	13,096	71.8	14,366	75.7	14,440	67.9	78.1	4.5	13.4
Central Bank	2	0.01	2	0.01	2	0.01	0.01	(18.0)	(19.4)
Corporate	6,671	36.6	6,958	36.6	6,810	32.0	36.8	1.8	4.9
Hong Kong, China									
Total	388	101.5	384	95.3	403	100.0	98.5	4.9	3.3
Treasury and Other Government	36	9.5	29	7.1	39	9.7	9.5	36.6	6.6
Central Bank	161	42.1	167	41.4	168	41.8	41.1	0.9	4.1
Corporate	190	49.9	189	46.8	195	48.5	47.8	3.5	2.1
Indonesia									
Total	428	31.5	498	34.7	477	100.0	34.7	1.9	16.7
Treasury and Other Government	377	27.8	403	28.0	387	81.0	28.1	2.0	7.2
Central Bank	21	1.5	65	4.5	61	12.9	4.5	0.3	211.2
Corporate	30	2.2	30	2.1	29	6.1	2.1	3.4	2.6
Republic of Korea									
Total	2,497	134.0	2,504	130.9	2,241	100.0	129.4	0.2	2.5
Treasury and Other Government	933	50.0	954	49.8	847	37.8	48.9	(0.5)	3.8
Central Bank	94	5.1	87	4.5	79	3.5	1.9	1.6	(4.9)
Corporate	1,470	78.9	1,464	76.5	1,315	58.7	75.9	0.6	2.2
Malaysia									
Total	436	127.7	504	127.6	468	100.0	127.0	0.8	4.6
Treasury and Other Government	248	72.5	294	74.5	273	58.3	74.0	0.6	7.3
Central Bank	4	1.1	0	0.0	0	0.0	0.0	–	(100.0)
Corporate	184	54.0	210	53.1	195	41.7	53.0	1.0	3.1
Philippines									
Total	217	49.4	232	50.2	223	100.0	48.9	(0.6)	7.5
Treasury and Other Government	178	40.6	193	41.7	187	83.5	40.8	(0.1)	9.2
Central Bank	11	2.6	16	3.4	14	6.1	3.0	(11.7)	23.0
Corporate	27	6.2	24	5.1	23	10.5	5.1	2.6	(10.4)
Singapore									
Total	574	112.6	651	117.1	622	100.0	116.1	1.6	12.1
Treasury and Other Government	210	41.2	236	42.5	225	36.2	42.0	1.4	10.9
Central Bank	223	43.6	262	47.1	249	40.1	46.5	1.2	15.8
Corporate	142	27.8	153	27.6	148	23.8	27.6	2.5	7.9
Thailand									
Total	483	91.8	531	92.9	501	100.0	91.9	(0.1)	3.6
Treasury and Other Government	276	52.4	312	54.5	297	59.2	54.4	0.8	7.5
Central Bank	65	12.4	73	12.8	69	13.7	12.6	(0.8)	4.7
Corporate	142	27.0	146	25.5	136	27.1	24.9	(1.6)	(4.6)
Viet Nam									
Total	110	25.8	123	27.0	124	100.0	27.5	5.0	18.9
Treasury and Other Government	80	18.8	88	19.5	87	70.2	19.3	2.3	14.6
Central Bank	0	0.0	3	0.6	5	4.4	1.2	95.0	2,927.0
Corporate	30	6.9	31	6.9	32	25.4	7.0	4.4	12.0
Emerging East Asia									
Total	24,902	103.4	26,753	106.3	26,311	100.0	108.0	3.1	9.6
Treasury and Other Government	15,434	64.1	16,874	67.0	16,781	63.8	68.9	4.0	12.4
Central Bank	581	2.4	674	2.7	646	2.5	2.7	0.9	15.1
Corporate	8,887	36.9	9,205	36.6	8,884	33.8	36.5	1.6	4.3
Japan									
Total	9,670	230.4	9,636	229.4	8,853	100.0	228.4	0.5	2.0
Treasury and Other Government	8,918	212.5	8,876	211.3	8,154	92.1	210.3	0.6	1.9
Central Bank	27	0.6	25	0.6	20	0.2	0.5	(10.7)	(16.2)
Corporate	725	17.3	736	17.5	678	7.7	17.5	0.9	4.4

( ) = negative, – = not applicable, GDP = gross domestic product, Q3 = third quarter, Q4 = fourth quarter, q-o-q = quarter-on-quarter, USD = United States dollar, y-o-y = year-on-year.

Notes:

1. For Singapore, corporate bonds outstanding are based on *AsianBondsOnline* estimates.
2. GDP data are from CEIC Data Company.
3. Bloomberg LP end-of-period local currency–USD rates are used.
4. Growth rates are calculated from a local currency base and do not include currency effects. For emerging East Asia, growth figures are based on 31 December 2024 currency exchange rates and do not include currency effects.

Sources: People's Republic of China (CEIC Data Company); Hong Kong, China (Hong Kong Monetary Authority); Indonesia (Bank Indonesia; Directorate General of Budget Financing and Risk Management, Ministry of Finance; and Indonesia Stock Exchange); Japan (Japan Securities Dealers Association); Republic of Korea (Bank of Korea and KG Zeroin Corporation); Malaysia (Bank Negara Malaysia); Philippines (Bangko Sentral ng Pilipinas, Bureau of the Treasury, and Bloomberg LP); Singapore (Monetary Authority of Singapore and Bloomberg LP); Thailand (Bank of Thailand); and Viet Nam (Hanoi Stock Exchange, State Bank of Vietnam, Vietnam Bond Market Association, and Bloomberg LP).

Table A2: Local-Currency-Denominated Bond Issuance

	Q4 2023		Q3 2024		Q4 2024		Growth Rate (%)	
	Amount (USD billion)	% share	Amount (USD billion)	% share	Amount (USD billion)	% share	Q4 2024	
							q-o-q	y-o-y
People's Republic of China								
Total	1,565	100.0	1,974	100.0	1,652	100.0	(13.0)	8.5
Treasury and Other Government	946	60.4	1,190	60.3	953	57.7	(16.7)	3.5
Central Bank	0	0.0	0	0.0	0	0.0	–	–
Corporate	619	39.6	784	39.7	699	42.3	(7.3)	16.0
Hong Kong, China								
Total	158	100.0	164	100.0	181	100.0	10.4	14.0
Treasury and Other Government	4	2.5	0	0.1	11	5.9	5,451.8	173.0
Central Bank	129	81.9	133	81.2	134	74.3	0.9	3.3
Corporate	25	15.6	31	19	36	19.8	17.3	44.6
Indonesia								
Total	44	100.0	51	100.0	43	100.0	(10.5)	1.8
Treasury and Other Government	11	25.5	16	31.8	12	27.4	(22.9)	9.5
Central Bank	31	69.0	33	64.2	28	65.3	(9.0)	(3.8)
Corporate	2	5.5	2	4.0	3	7.3	62.2	36.2
Republic of Korea								
Total	232	100.0	184	100.0	194	100.0	18.0	(4.6)
Treasury and Other Government	32	14.0	43	23.5	28	14.4	(27.6)	(1.6)
Central Bank	17	7.5	16	8.5	14	7.4	2.5	(6.4)
Corporate	182	78.5	125	68.0	151	78.2	35.8	(5.0)
Malaysia								
Total	34	100.0	26	100.0	18	100.0	(23.5)	(48.0)
Treasury and Other Government	10	29.1	14	52.9	7	39.2	(43.4)	(30.0)
Central Bank	14	41.4	0	0.0	0	0.0	–	(100.0)
Corporate	10	29.4	12	47.1	11	60.8	(1.2)	7.5
Philippines								
Total	41	100.0	52	100.0	41	100.0	(19.2)	3.8
Treasury and Other Government	8	19.0	14	27.6	7	17.7	(48.2)	(3.2)
Central Bank	32	77.8	35	66.7	33	79.7	(3.4)	6.4
Corporate	1	3.2	3	5.7	1	2.6	(63.3)	(17.3)
Singapore								
Total	352	100.0	424	100.0	411	100.0	3.0	20.8
Treasury and Other Government	35	9.8	41	9.7	40	9.8	3.6	20.2
Central Bank	316	89.8	380	89.6	367	89.4	2.7	20.3
Corporate	1	0.4	3	0.7	3	0.8	30.4	142.5
Thailand								
Total	58	100.0	69	100.0	61	100.0	(5.7)	5.0
Treasury and Other Government	14	24.7	21	30.1	18	29.0	(9.4)	23.3
Central Bank	30	52.2	35	51.8	33	54.4	(1.0)	9.3
Corporate	13	23.1	12	18.1	10	16.6	(13.2)	(24.4)
Viet Nam								
Total	18	100.0	40	100.0	37	100.0	(6.0)	114.7
Treasury and Other Government	3	15.8	5	11.6	2	6.3	(49.0)	(14.3)
Central Bank	11	62.4	31	77.9	30	82.7	(0.2)	184.5
Corporate	4	21.8	4	10.5	4	11.0	(1.7)	8.4
Emerging East Asia								
Total	2,502	100.0	2,983	100.0	2,637	100.0	(7.5)	9.2
Treasury and Other Government	1,063	42.5	1,344	45.1	1,078	40.9	(16.3)	4.5
Central Bank	580	23.2	663	22.2	640	24.3	1.1	13.2
Corporate	858	34.3	976	32.7	919	34.8	(1.2)	12.2
Japan								
Total	431	100.0	379	100.0	340	100.0	(1.9)	(12.1)
Treasury and Other Government	389	90.2	343	90.4	301	88.6	(3.9)	(13.6)
Central Bank	14	3.3	0	0.0	11	3.2	–	(14.6)
Corporate	28	6.5	36	9.6	28	8.2	(15.3)	10.7

( ) = negative, – = not applicable, Q3 = third quarter, Q4 = fourth quarter, q-o-q = quarter-on-quarter, USD = United States dollar, y-o-y = year-on-year.

Notes:

1. Data reflect gross bond issuance.
2. Bloomberg LP end-of-period local currency–USD rates are used.
3 Growth rates are calculated from a local currency base and do not include currency effects. For emerging East Asia, growth figures are based on 31 December 2024 currency exchange rates and do not include currency effects.

Sources: People's Republic of China (CEIC Data Company); Hong Kong, China (Hong Kong Monetary Authority); Indonesia (Bank Indonesia, Directorate General of Budget Financing and Risk Management, Ministry of Finance; and Indonesia Stock Exchange); Japan (Japan Securities Dealers Association); Republic of Korea (Bank of Korea and KG Zeroin Corporation); Malaysia (Bank Negara Malaysia); Philippines (Bangko Sentral ng Pilipinas, Bureau of the Treasury, and Bloomberg LP); Singapore (Monetary Authority of Singapore and Bloomberg LP); Thailand (Bank of Thailand and Thai Bond Market Association); and Viet Nam (Hanoi Stock Exchange, State Bank of Vietnam, Vietnam Bond Market Association, and Bloomberg LP).

Recent Developments in the ASEAN+3 Sustainable Bond Market

Sustainable Bonds Outstanding

Sustainable bonds outstanding in ASEAN+3 markets expanded to USD917.6 billion at the end of 2024 amid a slowdown in annual issuance.[10] Year-on-year (y-o-y) growth eased to 12.1% in 2024, down from 29.4% in 2023, tracking global growth moderation to 15.2% in 2024, down from 22.2% in 2023. ASEAN+3's sustainable bond market growth outpaced that of the United States (6.2% y-o-y) but lagged that of the European Union 20 (EU-20) (15.2%). ASEAN+3's share of the global sustainable bond market slightly dipped to 18.9% in 2024 from 19.4% in 2023 as the second-largest market globally, following the EU-20's 36.6% share (**Figure 10**). ASEAN+3's sustainable bond market size of USD917.6 billion in 2024 reflected a nearly sixfold increase from USD158.6 billion in 2018. Despite this expansion, ASEAN+3's sustainable bond market accounted for only 2.3% of the region's general bond market at the end of 2024, trailing the EU-20's corresponding share of 8.1%. Within ASEAN+3, the fastest growing sustainable bond markets were those of Japan and the Association of Southeast Asian Nations (ASEAN), with y-o-y growth rates of 26.6% and 25.4%, respectively, in 2024.

At the end of 2024, the ASEAN+3 sustainable bond market largely comprised green bonds, private sector issuances, and local currency (LCY) financing (Figure 11). Some improvements in the diversity of ASEAN+3's sustainable bonds were observed in 2024, with the share of green bonds falling to 59.1% at the end of December from 63.0% a year earlier. In contrast, the EU-20's share of green bonds to total sustainable bonds outstanding stood at 65.7%. ASEAN+3 has relatively

Figure 10: Global Sustainable Bonds Outstanding

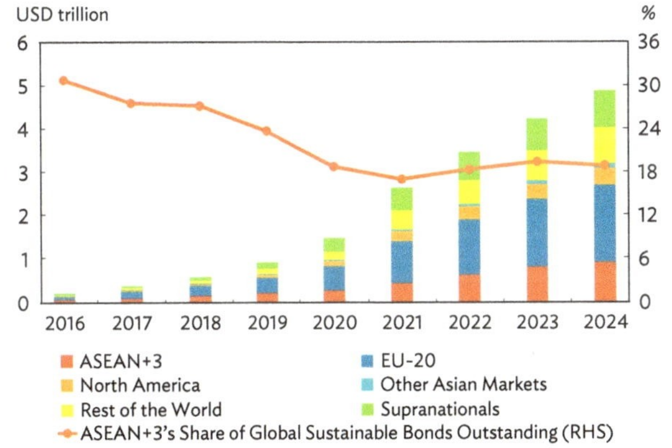

ASEAN+3 = Association of Southeast Asian Nations plus the People's Republic of China; Hong Kong, China; Japan; and the Republic of Korea; EU-20 = European Union 20; RHS = right-hand side; USD = United States dollar.

Notes:

1. The EU-20 includes EU member markets Austria, Belgium, Croatia, Cyprus, Estonia, Finland, France, Germany, Greece, Ireland, Italy, Latvia, Lithuania, Luxembourg, Malta, the Netherlands, Portugal, Slovakia, Slovenia, and Spain.
2. Data include both local currency and foreign currency issues.

Source: *AsianBondsOnline* calculations based on Bloomberg LP data.

Figure 11: Market Profile of Outstanding ASEAN+3 Sustainable Bonds at the End of 2024

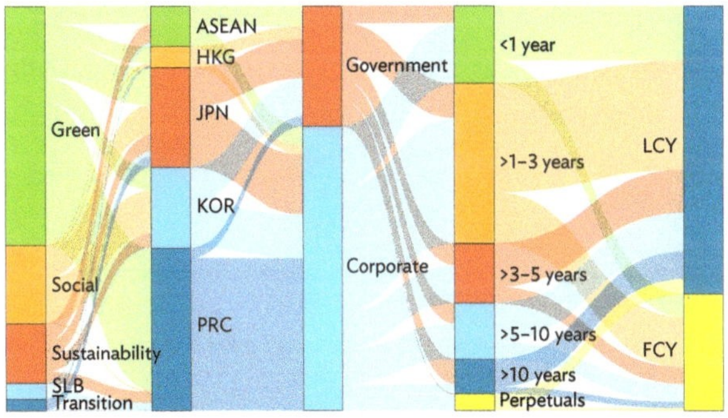

ASEAN = Association of Southeast Asian Nations; PRC = People's Republic of China; FCY = foreign currency; HKG = Hong Kong, China; JPN = Japan; KOR = Republic of Korea; LCY = local currency; SLB = sustainability-linked bond.

Notes:

1. ASEAN+3 is defined to include member states of ASEAN plus the People's Republic of China; Hong Kong, China; Japan; and the Republic of Korea.
2. ASEAN comprises the markets of Cambodia, Indonesia, the Lao People's Democratic Republic, Malaysia, the Philippines, Singapore, Thailand, and Viet Nam.
3. SLBs include transition-linked bonds.

Source: *AsianBondsOnline* calculations based on Bloomberg LP data.

[10] ASEAN+3 is defined to include member states of ASEAN plus the People's Republic of China; Hong Kong, China; Japan; and the Republic of Korea.

more transition bond issuance, with outstanding transition bonds accounting for 2.8% of the total sustainable bond stock, compared with a corresponding share of only 0.3% in the EU-20 (**Table**). Public sector participation in ASEAN+3 sustainable bonds remained low. Only 29.8% of sustainable bonds outstanding at the end of 2024 had been issued by the public sector, compared with the EU-20's 48.8% share. In contrast, ASEAN+3's public sector accounted for 75.2% of all general bonds outstanding at the end of December. Within ASEAN+3, the public sector accounted for the largest share of the sustainable bond market in Hong Kong, China (59.6%) and in ASEAN economies (51.5%). In ASEAN+3, the average LCY financing share in the region's sustainable bond market was 71.2% at the end of 2024, compared with 95.3% in the region's general bond market. In the EU-20, however, the LCY financing shares in the sustainable and general bond markets are more comparable at 90.2% and 89.5%, respectively.

Table: Instrument, Issuer, and Currency Profiles in the ASEAN+3 and European Union 20 Sustainable Bond Markets at the End of 2024 (%)

By End-2024	ASEAN+3	EU-20
Instrument profile (as a share of regional sustainable bonds outstanding)		
Green bonds	59.1	65.7
Social bonds	19.3	17.1
Sustainability bonds	14.8	9.2
SLBs (including transition-linked bonds)	4.0	7.8
Transition bonds	2.8	0.3
Issuer and currency profile		
Private sector (as a share of regional general bonds outstanding)	24.8	39.9
Private sector (as a share of regional sustainable bonds outstanding)	70.2	51.2
LCY financing (as a share of regional general bonds outstanding)	95.3	89.5
LCY financing (as a share of regional sustainable bonds outstanding)	71.2	90.2

ASEAN+3 = Association of Southeast Asian Nations plus the People's Republic of China; Hong Kong, China; Japan; and the Republic of Korea; EU-20 = European Union 20; LCY = local currency; SLB = sustainability-linked bond.

Source: *AsianBondsOnline* calculations based on Bloomberg LP data.

ASEAN+3 sustainable bonds outstanding at the end of 2024 mostly comprised short- to medium-term financing. Around 73.5% of ASEAN+3's sustainable bonds outstanding at the end of December had remaining tenors of 5 years or less, which was a much larger share than the EU-20's 42.9%. This resulted in a size-weighted average tenor of 4.5 years, nearly half of the EU-20's average of 8.3 years (**Figure 12**). The maturity structure of ASEAN sustainable bonds is closer to that of the EU-20, with 64.0% of outstanding sustainable bonds in ASEAN economies at the end of December carrying remaining maturities longer than 5 years. ASEAN outstanding sustainable bonds had a size-weighted average tenor of 11.2 years, exceeding the EU-20's 8.3 years. The prevalence of longer-tenor bonds in ASEAN markets is largely due to the active participation of the public sector, with the government regularly issuing sustainable bonds in Indonesia, the Philippines, Singapore, and Thailand. By instrument type, green bonds and social bonds mostly carried short-term tenors at the end of 2024, with 77.2% and 79.0% of ASEAN+3's outstanding green and social bonds, respectively, carrying remaining tenors of 5 years or less, compared with corresponding shares of 39.7% and 52.6%, respectively, in the EU-20 (**Figure 13**).

Figure 12: Maturity Profiles of ASEAN+3 and European Union 20 Sustainable Bonds Outstanding at the End of 2024

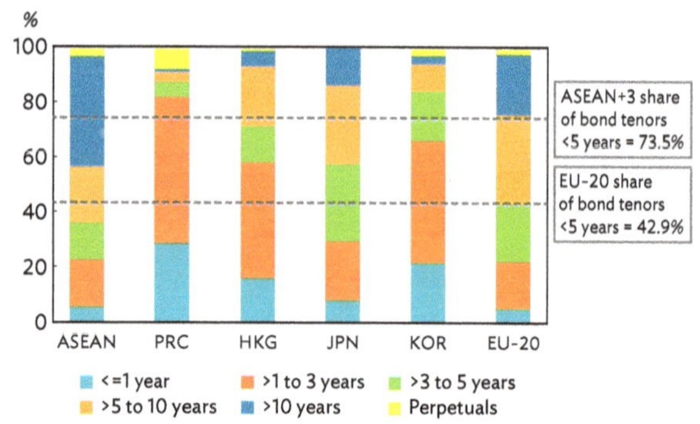

ASEAN = Association of Southeast Asian Nations; PRC = People's Republic of China; EU-20 = European Union 20; HKG = Hong Kong, China; JPN = Japan; KOR = Republic of Korea.

Notes:

1. ASEAN+3 is defined to include member states of ASEAN plus the People's Republic of China; Hong Kong, China; Japan; and the Republic of Korea.
2. ASEAN comprises the markets of Cambodia, Indonesia, the Lao People's Democratic Republic, Malaysia, the Philippines, Singapore, Thailand, and Viet Nam.
3. The EU-20 includes European Union member markets Austria, Belgium, Croatia, Cyprus, Estonia, Finland, France, Germany, Greece, Ireland, Italy, Latvia, Lithuania, Luxembourg, Malta, the Netherlands, Portugal, Slovakia, Slovenia, and Spain.
4. Data include both local currency and foreign currency issues.

Source: *AsianBondsOnline* calculations based on Bloomberg LP data.

Figure 13: Maturity Profiles of ASEAN+3 and European Union 20 Sustainable Bonds Outstanding by Type of Bond at the End of 2024

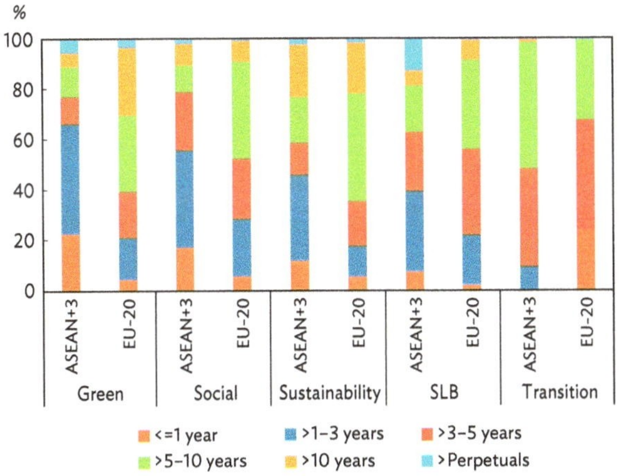

ASEAN+3 = Association of Southeast Asian Nations plus the People's Republic of China; Hong Kong, China; Japan; and the Republic of Korea; EU-20 = European Union 20; SLB = sustainability-linked bond.

Notes:

1. The EU-20 includes EU member markets Austria, Belgium, Croatia, Cyprus, Estonia, Finland, France, Germany, Greece, Ireland, Italy, Latvia, Lithuania, Luxembourg, Malta, the Netherlands, Portugal, Slovakia, Slovenia, and Spain.
2. Data include both local currency and foreign currency issues.
3. SLBs include transition-linked bonds.

Source: *AsianBondsOnline* computations based on Bloomberg LP data.

Figure 14: ASEAN+3 Sustainable Bond Issuance and Share of the Global Total

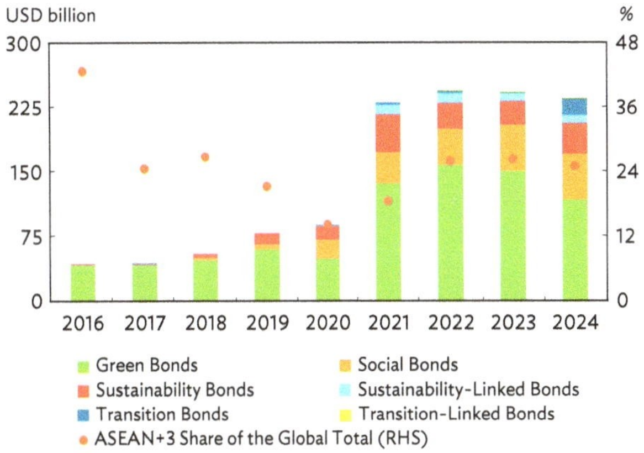

ASEAN+3 = Association of Southeast Asian Nations plus the People's Republic of China; Hong Kong, China; Japan; and the Republic of Korea; RHS = right-hand side; USD = United States dollar.

Notes:

1. Data include both local currency and foreign currency issues.
2. Sustainability-linked bonds include transition-linked bonds.

Source: *AsianBondsOnline* calculations based on Bloomberg LP data.

Sustainable Bond Issuance

ASEAN+3 sustainable bond issuance fell to USD237.2 billion in 2024 on a 3.1% y-o-y contraction, amid lingering high interest rates and expectations of policy shifts in the United States (US). The pace of contraction, however, was slower compared to that in the EU-20 where sustainable bond issuance declined 9.0% y-o-y in 2024. Despite a contraction in issuance, the EU-20 and ASEAN+3 remained the largest issuers of sustainable bonds in the world, accounting for global shares of 30.2% and 25.2%, respectively (**Figure 14**). During the year, the slowdown in ASEAN+3's issuance was due to a decline in the issuance of green bonds, which were down 21.8% y-o-y, and social bonds, which fell 1.4% y-o-y. On the other hand, the issuance of transition bonds accelerated rapidly by 1,170.0% y-o-y and sustainability bond issuance increased 29.4% y-o-y during the same period. The PRC accounted for 39.5% of total regional sustainable bond issuance in 2024 and 63.4% of regional green bond issuance. The PRC and ASEAN markets accounted for 36.0% and 30.0% of regional sustainability bond issuance, respectively. The Republic of Korea issued around 53.5% of regional social bonds, while Japan issued nearly all of the region's transition bonds.

Figure 15: Market Profile of ASEAN+3 Sustainable Bond Issuance in 2024

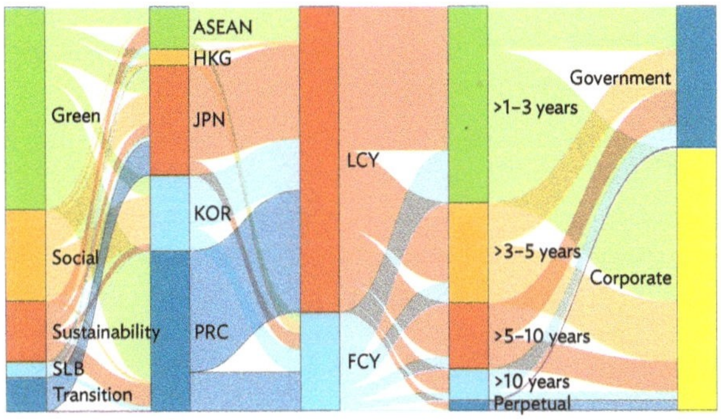

ASEAN = Association of Southeast Asian Nations; PRC = People's Republic of China; FCY = foreign currency; HKG = Hong Kong, China; JPN = Japan; KOR = Republic of Korea; LCY = local currency; SLB = sustainability-linked bond.

Notes:

1. ASEAN+3 is defined to include member states of ASEAN plus the People's Republic of China; Hong Kong, China; Japan; and the Republic of Korea.
2. ASEAN comprises the markets of Cambodia, Indonesia, Malaysia, the Philippines, Singapore, Thailand, and Viet Nam.
3. SLBs include transition-linked bonds.

Source: *AsianBondsOnline* calculations based on Bloomberg LP data.

Consistent with the market profile for outstanding bonds, ASEAN+3's sustainable bond issuance in 2024 remained denominated by LCY, short- and medium-term, and private sector financing (Figure 15).

- Around 75.5% of ASEAN+3 sustainable bond issuance in 2024 was in a local currency, which was lower than the LCY financing share of 95.6% for general bond issuance. In ASEAN economies, however, the LCY issuance shares in the sustainable bond market (79.3%) and general bond market (80.6%) were broadly similar in 2024. Meanwhile, in the EU-20, the LCY share of its sustainable bond issuance (86.6%) exceeded the corresponding share for general bond market issuance (78.0%) in 2024.

- Around 73.3% of ASEAN+3's sustainable bond issuance during the year carried tenors of 5 years or less, compared with a much lower share of 43.5% for ASEAN markets. The size-weighted average tenor of sustainable bond issuance in ASEAN was 12.3 years, more than double the 6.0 years for ASEAN+3 and higher than the 9.0 years for the EU-20. The relatively higher share of longer-term sustainable bond financing in ASEAN is largely driven by the active participation of the public sector, which accounted for 75.8% of sustainable bond issuance with tenors of over 5 years in 2024.
- Around 65.1% of sustainable bonds issued in ASEAN+3 in 2024 were from the private sector, contrasting with the private sector's share of 35.4% in the region's general bond market. The public sector has a strong presence in transition bond issuance, representing 88.0% of ASEAN+3's transition bond issuance in 2024, and in social bond issuance (57.4%). The private sector led in the issuance of sustainability-linked bonds (90.2% of regional issuance), green bonds (79.9%), and sustainability bonds (71.9%). Among private sector issuers, the largest issuance shares belonged to the financial sector (42.8%), industrials (18.1%), and utilities (13.4%).

Figure 16: ASEAN+3 Sustainable Bond Issuance by Sector in 2024

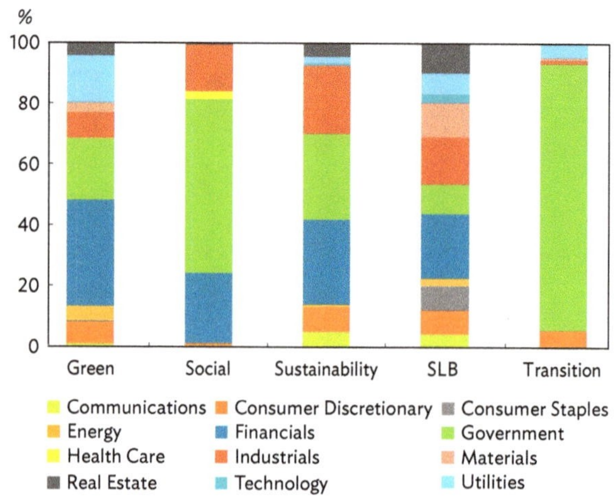

SLB = sustainability-linked bond.

Notes:

1. ASEAN+3 is defined to include member states of the Association of Southeast Asian Nations plus the People's Republic of China; Hong Kong, China; Japan; and the Republic of Korea.
2. Data include both local currency and foreign currency issues.
3. SLBs include transition-linked bonds.

Source: *AsianBondsOnline* computations based on Bloomberg LP data.

Liquidity Conditions in Emerging East Asian Local Currency Bond Market

Overview

Liquidity in emerging east Asia generally improved in 2024, supported by monetary policy easing.[11] Average bid–ask spreads for local currency (LCY) government bonds narrowed in 2024 from the previous year for both on-the-run and off-the run issues, while they were largely unchanged for corporate bonds. Average issuance sizes for both government and corporate bonds also increased for most markets in the region. In 2024, average turnover ratios for government bonds rose, indicating increased trading activities, while corporate bond turnover ratios were steady.

Government Bond Markets

LCY government bond bid–ask spreads narrowed in most emerging East Asian markets in 2024. Most regional government bond markets saw declines in their respective bid–ask spreads in 2024, buoyed by easing monetary stances both in the region and in advanced economies amid moderating inflation. Average bid–ask spreads for on-the-run LCY government bonds in the region narrowed to 5.7 basis points (bps) in 2024 from 7.4 bps in 2023, with six out of nine markets recorded lower bid–ask spreads in 2024 than in the previous year (**Figure 17A**). Among regional markets, Viet Nam's government bonds showed the largest decline in bid–ask spreads, driven by increased government bond issuance. Meanwhile, government bond bid–ask spreads in some regional markets—such as the People's Republic of China (PRC), the Philippines, and Thailand—remained stable or slightly widened. Market liquidity tightened somewhat due to risks associated with the change in government in Thailand and concerns over slowing economic growth in the PRC. Bid–ask spreads for off-the-run LCY government bonds in the region generally narrowed during the review period (**Figure 17B**). The region's average bid–ask spreads for off-the-run government bonds narrowed to 6.2 bps in 2024 from 7.5 bps in the previous year.

Figure 17: Average Bid–Ask Spreads for Local Currency Government Bonds

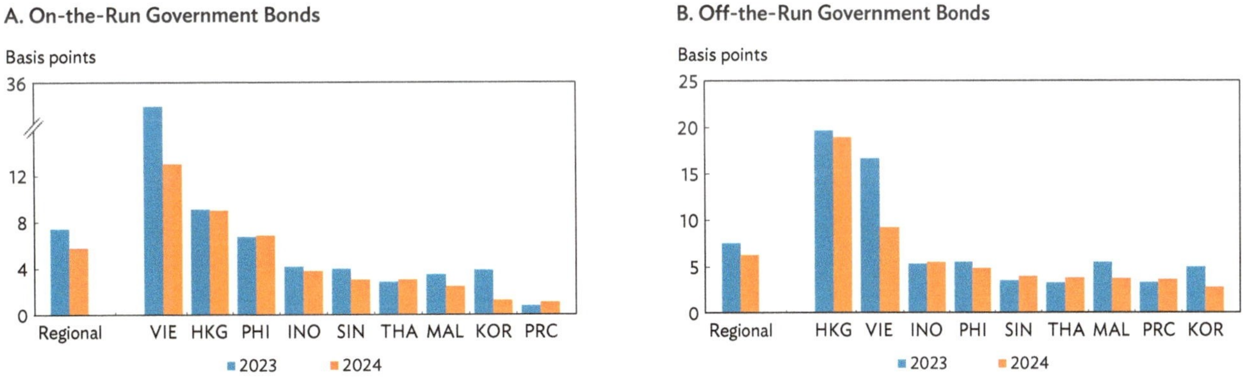

PRC = People's Republic of China; HKG = Hong Kong, China; INO = Indonesia; KOR = Republic of Korea; MAL = Malaysia; PHI = Philippines; SIN = Singapore; THA = Thailand; VIE = Viet Nam.

Note: The regional bid–ask spread refers to the average spread of the nine markets of emerging East Asia.

Source: *AsianBondsOnline* calculations based on Bloomberg LP data.

11 Emerging East Asia is defined to include member states of the Association of Southeast Asian Nations (ASEAN) plus the People's Republic of China; Hong Kong, China; and the Republic of Korea.

The average issuance size for LCY government bonds in the region saw a slight uptick in 2024 amid the easing monetary environment. In 2024, the region's average issue size inched up marginally to USD2.2 billion from USD2.1 billion in 2023, with most markets showing slightly higher or similar average issuance sizes compared to 2023 (**Figure 18**). The PRC recorded the most significant increase in its average government bond issuance size, climbing to USD12.2 billion in 2024 from USD11.2 billion in 2023. The uptick was largely driven by the government's need to fund various stimulus measures and support the economy amid weak growth.

Figure 18: Average Issue Sizes of Local Currency Government Bonds

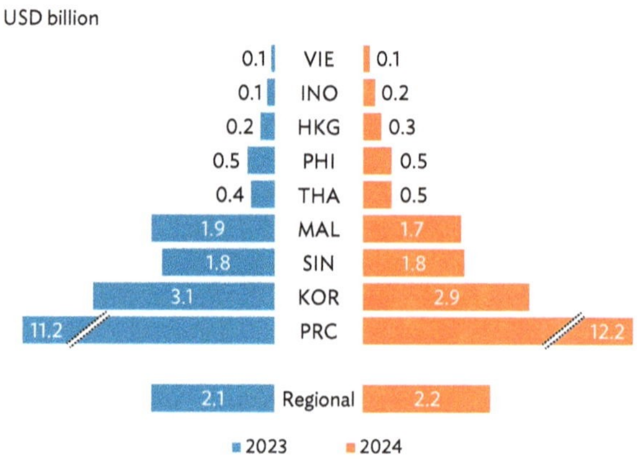

PRC = People's Republic of China; HKG = Hong Kong, China; INO = Indonesia; KOR = Republic of Korea; MAL = Malaysia; PHI = Philippines; SIN = Singapore; THA = Thailand; USD = United States dollar; VIE = Viet Nam.

Note: The regional average issue size refers to the average issue size of the nine markets of emerging East Asia.

Sources: *AsianBondsOnline* calculations based on various local market sources.

Turnover ratios for LCY government bonds rose in most regional markets in 2024. The simple average turnover ratio across the region in 2024 was 0.45, up from 0.36 in 2023 (**Figure 19**). The rise in turnover ratios was largely driven by increased trading activities due to expected and actual monetary policy easing by central banks across the region and in major advanced economies. In most regional markets, turnover ratios slightly fell in the last quarter of 2024 due to reduced bond issuance as governments had already front-loaded their budget financing needs. In the PRC, while the turnover ratio improved in 2024 overall, it steadily declined beginning in the second quarter of the year. This was partly because of the expanding base of outstanding bonds in 2024 as the government increased borrowings to support the economy, while annual trading volume climbed to CNY113.4 trillion from CNY68.8 trillion a year earlier. Another factor

Figure 19: Local Currency Government Bond Turnover Ratios in Select Emerging East Asian Markets

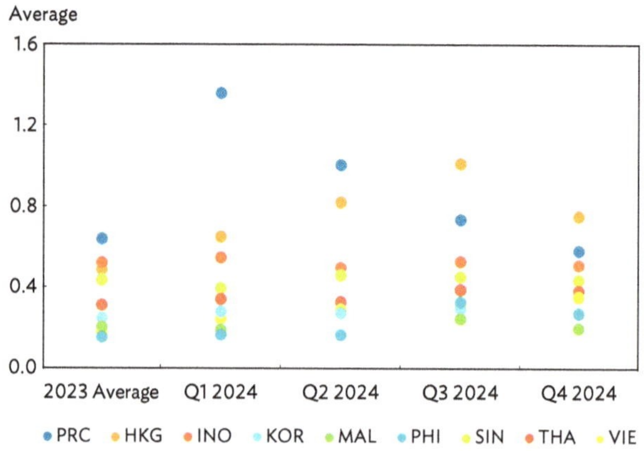

PRC = People's Republic of China; HKG = Hong Kong, China; INO = Indonesia; KOR = Republic of Korea; MAL = Malaysia; PHI = Philippines; Q1 = first quarter; Q2 = second quarter; Q3 = third quarter; Q4 = fourth quarter; SIN = Singapore; THA = Thailand; VIE = Viet Nam.

Notes:

1. Turnover ratios are calculated as the local currency trading volume (sales amount only) divided by the average local currency value of outstanding bonds during each 3-month period.
2. For the 2023 average, figures are based on the simple average of the quarterly turnover ratios of each market.

Sources: *AsianBondsOnline* calculations based on various local market sources.

contributing to the gradual decline of the turnover ratio in the PRC was the tightened regulatory oversight introduced in April when the central bank investigated the trading activities of some firms amid concerns over speculative trading as well as foreign outflows. The PRC posted continuous monthly bond outflows totaling USD36.3 billion from September through January.

Corporate Bond Markets

Bid-ask spreads for LCY corporate bonds were largely unchanged in emerging East Asia in 2024 compared with 2023. The region's simple average corporate bond bid-ask spread in 2024 was 16.8 bps, similar to 16.7 bps in 2023. Slight increases were noted in four out of seven corporate bond markets in the region in 2024 amid easing monetary stances in several markets. The average bid-ask spread for corporate bonds in the PRC widened the most, inching up to 18.1 bps in 2024 from 17.3 bps in 2023, largely due to the negative sentiments generated by bond defaults and the weak domestic economy (**Figure 20**). The corporate bond market in the Philippines continued to have the highest bid-ask spread in the region as its market is largely concentrated among a few large issuers. At the end of 2024, the top 30 corporate issuers comprised 94.1% of the Philippine corporate bond market.

Figure 20: Average Bid–Ask Spreads for Local Currency Corporate Bonds

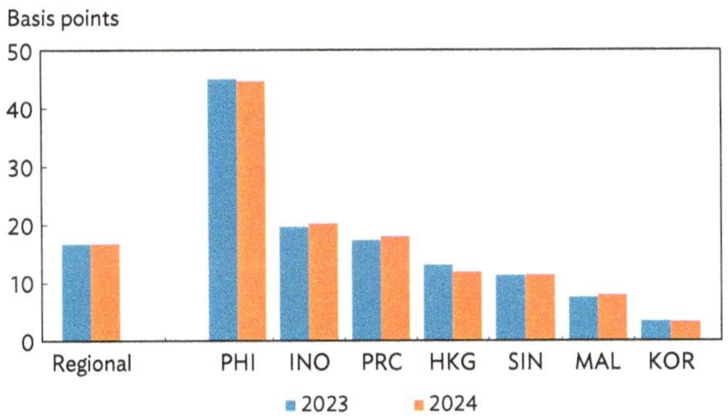

PRC = People's Republic of China; HKG = Hong Kong, China; INO = Indonesia; KOR = Republic of Korea; MAL = Malaysia; PHI = Philippines; SIN = Singapore.

Note: The regional bid–ask spread refers to the average spread of the nine markets of emerging East Asia.

Source: *AsianBondsOnline* calculations based on Bloomberg LP data.

Figure 21: Average Issue Sizes for Local Currency Corporate Bonds

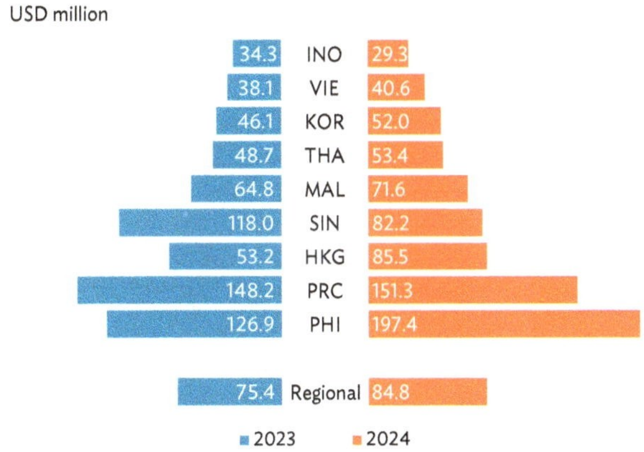

PRC = People's Republic of China; HKG = Hong Kong, China; INO = Indonesia; KOR = Republic of Korea; MAL = Malaysia; PHI = Philippines; SIN = Singapore; THA = Thailand; USD = United States dollar; VIE = Viet Nam.

Note: The regional average issue size refers to the average issue size of the nine markets of emerging East Asia.

Sources: *AsianBondsOnline* calculations based on various local market sources.

The average issue size of LCY corporate bonds in emerging East Asia increased in 2024 on improved financial conditions. The regional average issue size rose to USD84.8 million in 2024 from the previous year's USD75.4 million (**Figure 21**). The Philippines and the PRC had significantly higher average issue sizes at USD197.4 million and USD151.3 million, respectively. Corporations in the Philippines averaged higher issue sizes in 2024 versus 2023, driven by a few large-ticket issuances by SMC Tollways (PHP35.0 billion) and Security Bank (PHP20.0 billion), particularly in the second half of the year following a series of rate cuts by the Bangko Sentral ng Pilipinas starting in August. In the PRC, increased issue sizes in 2024 were driven by the capital-raising activities of banks and financial institutions aiming to meet the regulatory capital requirements that took effect at the start of the year to bring domestic banks in line with Basel III.

The regional average LCY corporate bond turnover ratio was largely similar in 2024 (0.14) as it was in 2023 (0.15). Among regional markets where data are available, the PRC saw the largest decline in its average LCY corporate bond turnover ratio in 2024 as the ratio edged down in the first 3 quarters of 2024 amid a weakening economy and continued concerns over bond defaults in the property sector (**Figure 22**). The turnover ratio for PRC corporate bonds subsequently recovered in the fourth quarter of 2024 on upbeat sentiment following government announcements of economic and property market stimulus measures in September and October. Meanwhile, the corporate bond turnover ratio in Hong Kong, China increased in 2024, buoyed by monetary easing, as it widely tracks monetary policy changes in the United States. Most other regional markets had largely stable turnover ratios in 2024 compared with 2023.

Figure 22: Local Currency Corporate Bond Turnover Ratios in Select Emerging East Asian Markets

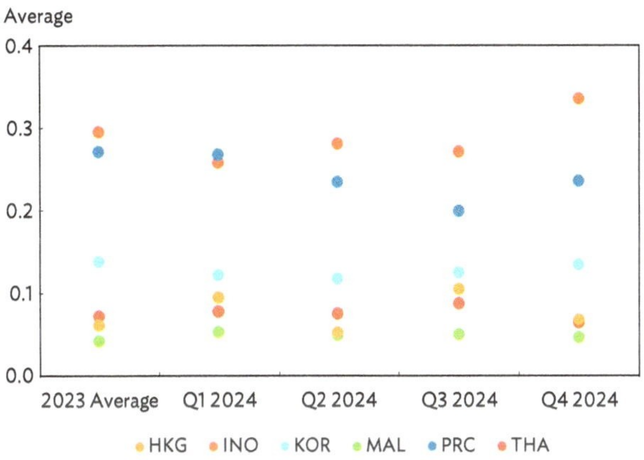

PRC = People's Republic of China; HKG = Hong Kong, China; INO = Indonesia; KOR = Republic of Korea; MAL = Malaysia; Q1 = first quarter; Q2 = second quarter; Q3 = third quarter; Q4 = fourth quarter; THA = Thailand.

Notes:

1. Turnover ratios are calculated as the local currency trading volume (sales amount only) divided by the average local currency value of outstanding bonds during each 3-month period.
2. For the 2023 average, figures are based on the simple average of the quarterly turnover ratios of each market.

Sources: *AsianBondsOnline* calculations based on various local market sources.

Policy and Regulatory Developments

People's Republic of China

People's Bank of China Suspends Bond Purchases

In January, the People's Bank of China announced that it would temporarily suspend central bank purchases of government bonds. In its decision, the central bank said the suspension would help reduce excess demand for government bonds. The central bank will resume purchases once it feels demand and supply conditions have stabilized.

Hong Kong, China

Hong Kong Monetary Authority Announces Revised Government Bond Issuance Plan

On 9 January, the Hong Kong Monetary Authority published a revised tentative schedule for institutional government bonds to be issued under the Infrastructure Bond Programme and the Government Sustainable Bond Programme during the first quarter of 2025. Compared with the previous issuance schedule published in October, the new schedule increased the planned amount of HKD-denominated government bonds to be issued in the first quarter of 2025 to HKD7.5 billion from HKD3.5 billion. Similarly, the planned issuance size of CNY-denominated government bonds was raised to CNY7.5 billion from CNY4.5 billion. The changes in the revised issuance schedule included two additional HKD-denominated tenders (3-year and 5-year bonds) and one additional CNY-denominated tender (10-year bond), as well as increases in the tentative issuance sizes of select tenders.

Indonesia

Bank Indonesia to Purchase IDR150 Trillion Worth of Government Bonds in 2025

In December, Bank Indonesia announced plans to purchase up to IDR150 trillion worth of government bonds from the secondary market in 2025. The bond purchase forms part of the central bank's monetary operations. Bank Indonesia utilizes government bonds as underlying assets for its issuance of short-term securities to attract foreign fund inflows and support the stability of the domestic currency. From the start of the year through 17 February, Bank Indonesia purchased a total of IDR32.5 trillion from the primary market (IDR13.0 trillion) and the secondary market (IDR19.5 trillion).

Republic of Korea

The Government of the Republic of Korea Announces 2025 Economic Outlook and Policy Directions

In January, the Government of the Republic of Korea announced its 2025 economic outlook and policy directions. Annual economic growth for 2024 and 2025 is projected to be 2.1% and 1.8%, respectively. The lower growth projection for the year is due to slow export growth affected by policy shifts in the United States, along with weak construction activity and economic sentiment. Meanwhile, inflation is expected to decelerate to 1.8% in 2025 due to lower oil prices, but uncertainty stemming from geopolitical risks remains. The policy direction for 2025 is focused on (i) supporting the recovery of people's livelihoods, (ii) managing external creditworthiness, (iii) proactively responding to uncertainties in the international trade environment, and (iv) increasing industrial competitiveness.

Malaysia

Regional Central Banks Collaborate on Framework for Cross-Border Transactions

On 17 February, Bank Negara Malaysia, along with Bank Indonesia and the Bank of Thailand, announced additional considerations for eligible transactions in the implementation of its Local Currency Transaction Framework Operational Guidelines. The transaction framework is a set of standards to enhance efficiencies in trade and investment among the three economies. It was previously revised in August 2023 to include cross-border financial transactions. Among the augmented guidelines, eligible cross-border transactions were expanded and portfolio investments are now eligible under the framework. These guidelines aim to streamline processes and improve transparency for key participating financial institutions. This collaboration reaffirms the participating economies' commitment to the use of local currencies in regional trade and investment.

Philippines

Bangko Sentral ng Pilipinas Cuts Reserve Requirement Ratio

On 21 February, the Bangko Sentral ng Pilipinas announced reductions to the reserve requirement ratio for banks effective 28 March. The reserve requirement ratio for banks and nonbank financial institutions will be lowered by 200 basis points (bps) to 5.0%, digital banks by 150 bps to 2.5%, and thrift banks by 100 bps to 0.0%. The adjustments are expected to reduce the obstacles in financial intermediation to facilitate improved liquidity conditions and provide the central bank with the flexibility to gradually lower interest rates.

Singapore

The Government of Singapore Increases Issuance Limit on Government Bonds

On 12 November, the Parliament of Singapore approved an increase in the issuance limit on government bonds to SGD1.5 trillion from SGD1.1 trillion, which was previously approved in January 2021. Over 60% of the incremental amount will be allocated for the issuance of special government securities in accordance with the investment needs of Singapore's Central Provident Fund. The remaining 20% of the increase will be allotted for the issuance of Singapore government securities, Treasury bills, and Singapore savings bonds. The new issuance limit is expected to hold until 2029.

Thailand

Public Debt Management Office Conducts THB24 Billion Bond Switch Transactions

On 22 November, the Public Debt Management Office (PDMO) concluded bond switch transactions totaling THB24.2 billion. Investors participating in the transactions swapped eligible government bonds maturing shortly for eligible destination bonds with longer remaining maturities. The source bond had a remaining maturity of 1 year, while the six destination bonds had remaining maturities of 5–48 years. The bond switch supported the PDMO's debt management objectives by reducing the bunching of debt with 1–4 year maturities and increasing the liquidity of longer-term government bonds. The PDMO plans to conduct a total of THB140 billion in bond switch transactions in fiscal year 2025.

Viet Nam

Ministry of Finance Revises Disclosure Regulations for Bond Issuers

Effective 25 December, entities issuing private bonds domestically and internationally must comply with the updated information disclosure requirements specified in Circular 76 by the Ministry of Finance. The new circular requires disclosure on (i) pre-issuance information; (ii) bond offering results; (iii) extraordinary developments; and (iv) details on bond conversion, warrants, early buybacks, and swaps. Semiannual and annual updates are also required. Issuers must communicate this information to investors via printed or electronic documents, or through their official websites, and this must be submitted electronically to the Hanoi Stock Exchange. Circular 76 aims to enhance transparency and accountability for bond issuers in both domestic and international markets. It replaces Circular 122 issued in December 2020.

Market Summaries

People's Republic of China

Yield Movements

Local currency (LCY) government bond yields in the People's Republic of China (PRC) fell for most tenors, particularly longer-dated ones, between 1 December 2024 and 28 February 2025 on expected further monetary easing by the central bank. Bond yields fell an average of 19 basis points (bps) for tenors of 5 years or more, while tenors of 4 years or less saw their yields rise an average of 12 bps (**Figure 1**). The decline in yields was supported by the Government of the PRC's announcement in December that it would implement more active fiscal policies and moderately loose monetary policies. This was further supported by the People's Bank of China's (PBOC) announcement in January that it planned to implement its moderately loose monetary policy sometime in 2025 by reducing interest rates and reserve requirement ratios. Meanwhile, continued low inflation due to weak domestic demand dragged down interest rates at the shorter end of the curve, with year-on-year consumer price inflation coming in at 0.5% in January and −0.7% in February, from 0.1% in December.

Local Currency Bond Market Size and Issuance

The PRC's LCY bonds outstanding grew at a slightly faster pace in the fourth quarter (Q4) of 2024 to reach CNY155.1 trillion at the end of December. Growth accelerated to 3.6% quarter-on-quarter (q-o-q) in Q4 2024 from 3.1% q-o-q in the previous quarter, led by faster q-o-q growth rates for both government bonds (4.5% versus 4.2%) and corporate bonds (1.8% versus 1.1%) (**Figure 2**). The faster growth in the government and corporate bond markets was driven by fewer maturities during the quarter.

Bond sales in the PRC declined to CNY12.1 trillion in Q4 2024 from CNY13.9 trillion in the third quarter of 2024, a 13.0% q-o-q decline. While issuance for both government and corporate bonds declined, it fell much faster for government bonds (−16.7% q-o-q) versus corporate bonds (−7.3% q-o-q) as the government had already met most of its annual borrowing requirements in the prior quarters (**Figure 3**).

Figure 1: The People's Republic of China's Benchmark Yield Curve—Local Currency Government Bonds

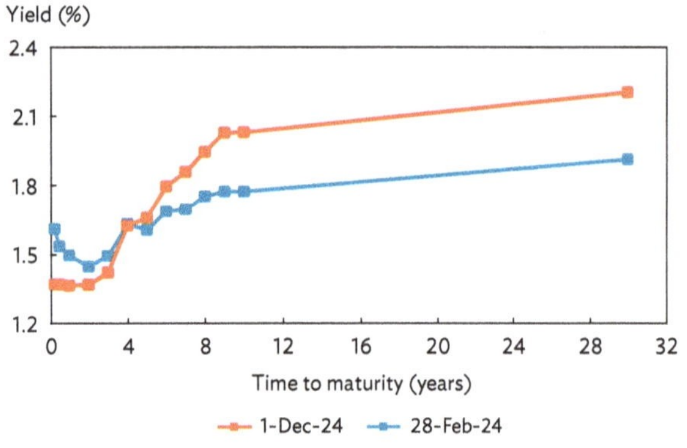

Source: Based on data from Bloomberg LP.

Figure 2: Composition of Local Currency Bonds Outstanding in the People's Republic of China

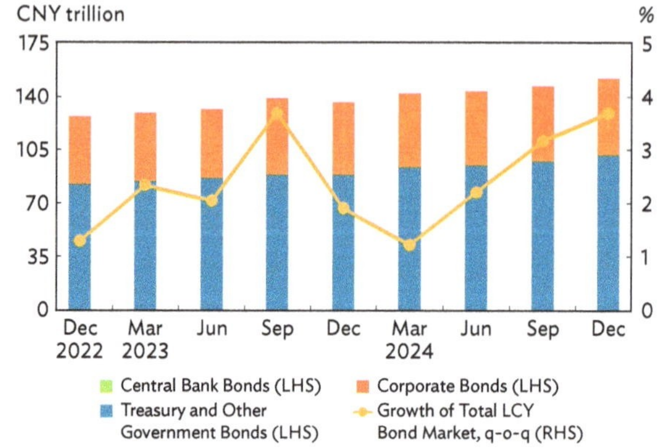

CNY = Chinese yuan, LCY = local currency, LHS = left-hand side, q-o-q = quarter-on-quarter, RHS = right-hand side.
Source: CEIC Data Company.

This market summary was written by Russ Jason Lo, consultant, Economic Research and Development Impact Department, Asian Development Bank, Manila.

Figure 3: Composition of Local Currency Bond Issuance in the People's Republic of China

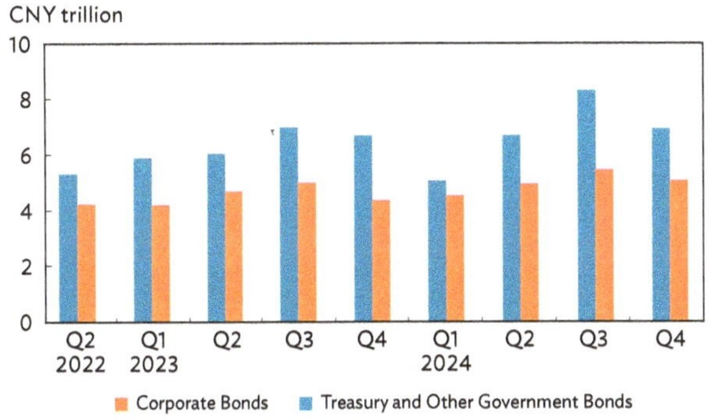

CNY = Chinese yuan, Q1 = first quarter, Q2 = second quarter, Q3 = third quarter, Q4 = fourth quarter.

Source: CEIC Data Company.

Investor Profile

The investor profile of the PRC's Treasury bond market remained roughly the same in 2024. There was a slight decline in the share of Treasury bonds held by banks to 66.6% at the end of December 2024 from 69.4% a year earlier (**Figure 4**). Banks, however, remained the dominant investor with other investors not elsewhere classified having the next largest share with only a 12.7% share. As a result of the large holdings share of banks, the PRC continued to have the second-highest Herfindahl–Hirschman Index score in emerging East Asia at the end of 2024, reflecting a less diverse investor profile.[12]

Figure 4: Investor Profile of Treasury Bonds

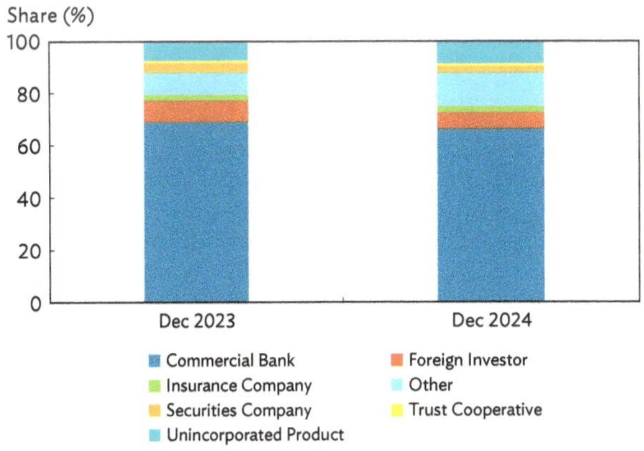

Source: CEIC Data Company.

Sustainable Bond Market

The PRC's sustainable bond market is dominated by green bond instruments and private sector financing. The PRC has the largest general bond market in emerging East Asia and also the largest sustainable bond market, which reached a size of USD368.1 billion and comprised 53.2% of the regional total at the end of December (**Figure 5**). A majority of the PRC's sustainable bonds are green bonds, with a share of 87.8%. The PRC bond market includes very few transition bonds at only USD0.9 billion, or a 0.2% share of the sustainable bond market. Private corporations are the most prevalent issuer of sustainable bonds, accounting for 93.9% of outstanding bonds. Most issuances are shorter-term, with 87.4% of outstanding sustainable bonds having a maturity of 5 years or less.

Figure 5: Market Profile of Outstanding Sustainable Bonds in the People's Republic of China at the End of December 2024

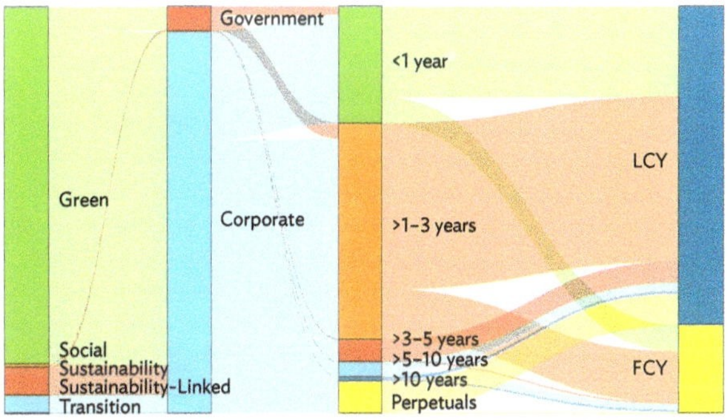

FCY = foreign currency, LCY = local currency.

Source: *AsianBondsOnline* calculations based on Bloomberg LP data.

12 The Herfindahl–Hirschman Index is a common measure of market concentration. The index is used to measure the investor profile diversification of the local currency bond market by summing the squared share of each investor group in the bond market. Emerging East Asia is defined to include member states of the Association of Southeast Asian Nations plus the People's Republic of China; Hong Kong, China; and the Republic of Korea.

Hong Kong, China

Yield Movements

Between 1 December 2024 and 28 February 2025, local currency (LCY) government bond yields in Hong Kong, China fell for most tenors. LCY government bond yields in Hong Kong, China fell for all maturities except the 3-year and 10-year bonds (**Figure 1**). The decline in LCY government bond yields largely tracked movements in United States Treasury yields, which fell on weaker economic data released in the latter half of February. Meanwhile, an increased supply of 3-year and 10-year government bonds from issuances under the Infrastructure Bond Programme in January and February drove yield hikes for the 3-year and 10-year bonds.

Figure 1: Hong Kong, China's Benchmark Yield Curve—Local Currency Government Bonds

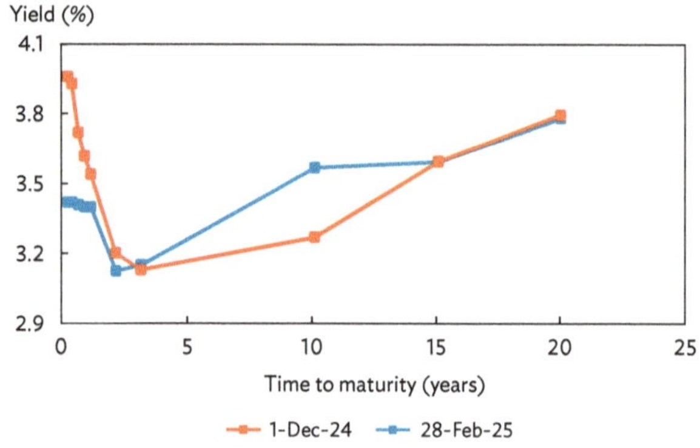

Source: Based on data from Bloomberg LP.

Local Currency Bond Market Size and Issuance

Hong Kong, China's LCY bond market rebounded in the fourth quarter (Q4) of 2024, supported by the robust growth of Hong Kong Special Administrative Region (HKSAR) government bonds. Outstanding LCY bonds reached HKD3.1 trillion at the end of December, expanding 4.9% quarter-on-quarter (q-o-q) in Q4 2024 after contracting 1.7% q-o-q in the previous quarter (**Figure 2**). Growth was led by a rebound in HKSAR government bonds, which rose 36.6% q-o-q in Q4 2024 due to a resurgence in issuance under the newly established Infrastructure Bond Programme. Expansions in outstanding corporate bonds and Exchange Fund Bills and Notes, which inched up 3.5% q-o-q and 0.9% q-o-q, respectively, also contributed to the overall market growth.

Figure 2: Composition of Local Currency Bonds Outstanding in Hong Kong, China

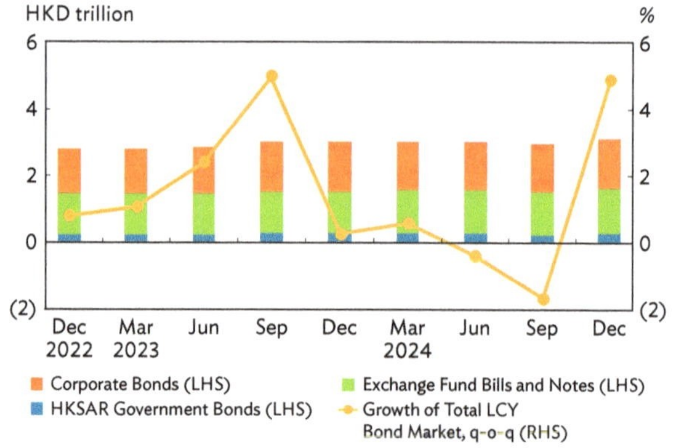

( ) = negative, HKD = Hong Kong dollar, HKSAR = Hong Kong Special Administrative Region, LCY = local currency, LHS = left-hand side, q-o-q = quarter-on-quarter, RHS = right-hand side.

Source: Hong Kong Monetary Authority.

This market summary was written by Debbie Gundaya, consultant, Economic Research and Development Impact Department, Asian Development Bank, Manila.

Total issuance of LCY bonds jumped 10.4% q-o-q in Q4 2024, fueled by increased issuance of HKSAR government bonds and corporate bonds. LCY bond issuance picked up in Q4 2024, totaling HKD1.4 trillion (**Figure 3**). Issuance of HKSAR government bonds, which jumped to HKD83.3 billion in Q4 2024 from HKD1.5 billion in the previous quarter, led the growth in aggregate LCY bond sales. Issuance under the new Infrastructure Bond Programme started during the quarter, including HKD10.5 billion worth of institutional bonds and HKD72.8 billion of retail bonds. Meanwhile, corporate bond sales also rebounded, rising 17.3% q-o-q in Q4 2024 after contracting 7.4% q-o-q in the preceding quarter on renewed investor optimism amid improved economic conditions. Hong Kong, China's gross domestic product growth rose to 2.4% year-on-year in Q4 2024 from 1.9% year-on-year in the third quarter of 2024, propped up by government spending and exports. Hong Kong Mortgage Corporation continued to top all nonbank issuers with total bond sales of HKD19.2 billion, accounting for 86.3% of total nonbank corporate issuances in Q4 2024.

Figure 3: Composition of Local Currency Bond Issuance in Hong Kong, China

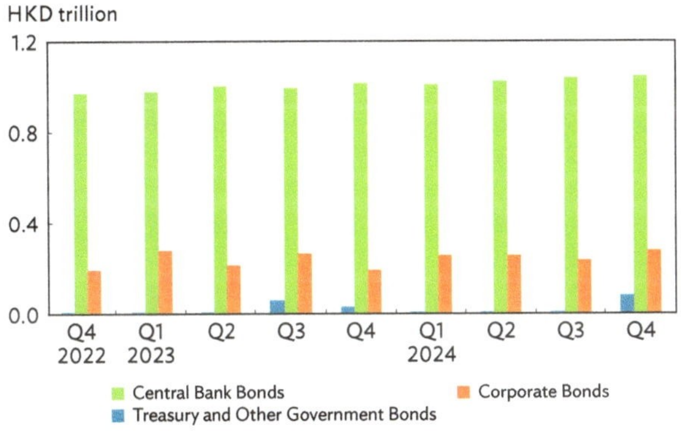

HKD = Hong Kong dollar, Q1 = first quarter, Q2 = second quarter, Q3 = third quarter, Q4 = fourth quarter.

Source: Hong Kong Monetary Authority.

Sustainable Bond Market

A majority of Hong Kong, China's sustainable bond market comprised green bond instruments issued by the public sector and denominated in a foreign currency. At the end of December, sustainable bonds outstanding totaled USD48.1 billion on growth of 3.2% q-o-q. Green bonds comprised nearly 80% of total sustainable bonds, followed by social bonds with a 12.9% share (**Figure 4**). Bonds issued by the public sector, which were all green bond instruments, comprised 59.6% of the total. Over 70% of outstanding sustainable bonds have remaining maturities of up to 5 years. Consequently, the size-weighted average tenor of outstanding sustainable bonds was 4.4 years at the end of December. Foreign-currency-denominated bonds comprised 76.8% of outstanding sustainable bonds in Hong Kong, China, the second-highest share among emerging East Asian markets, owing to the predominance of multi-currency government green bonds.[13] Meanwhile, social, sustainability, sustainability-linked, and transitions bonds were issued solely by the private sector. In Q4 2024, all sustainable bond issuances (USD3.0 billion) were social bonds from the private sector.

Figure 4: Market Profile of Outstanding Sustainable Bonds in Hong Kong, China at the End of December 2024

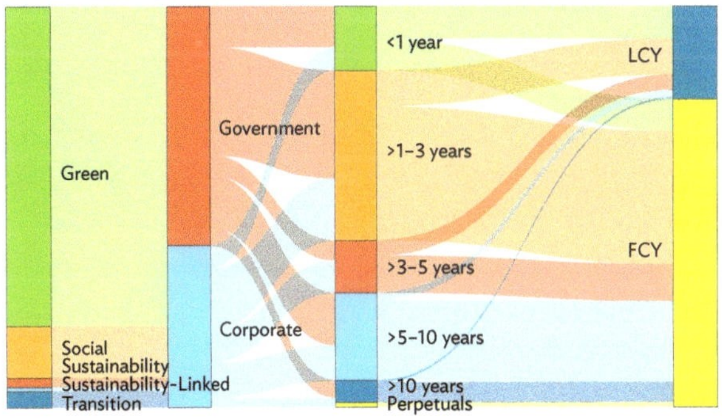

FCY = foreign currency, LCY = local currency.

Source: *AsianBondsOnline* calculations based on Bloomberg LP data.

[13] Emerging East Asia is defined to include member states of the Association of Southeast Asian Nations plus the People's Republic of China; Hong Kong, China; and the Republic of Korea.

Indonesia

Yield Movements

Between 1 December 2024 and 28 February 2025, the local currency (LCY) government bond yield curve in Indonesia shifted downward. Bond yields declined an average of 6 basis points (bps) across the curve, with yields for maturities of 2 years or less declining the most at an average of 12 bps (**Figure 1**). The downward shift in the yield curve was largely driven by Bank Indonesia's 25 bps rate cut in January to support economic growth. The central bank also slightly lowered its economic growth forecast for 2025 to a range of 4.7%–5.5% from an estimate of 4.8%–5.6% in December. In its February and March meetings, Bank Indonesia left the policy rate unchanged at 5.75% to ensure the stability of the Indonesian rupiah and to guide inflation toward the target range of 1.50%–3.50% amid heightened global uncertainties.

Figure 1: Indonesia's Benchmark Yield Curve—Local Currency Government Bonds

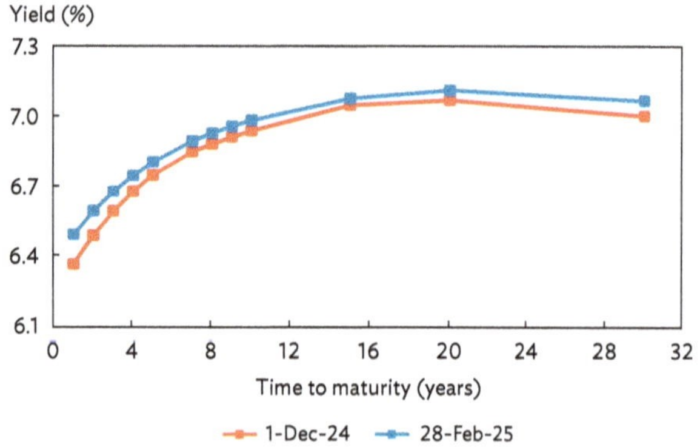

Source: Based on data from Bloomberg LP.

Local Currency Bond Market Size and Issuance

The LCY bond stock in Indonesia rose to IDR7,688.0 trillion at the end of December. Overall growth, however, slowed to 1.9% quarter-on-quarter (q-o-q) in the fourth quarter (Q4) of 2024 from 4.8% q-o-q in the third quarter (Q3) (**Figure 2**). Government bonds, which accounted for 81.0% of the total LCY bond stock at the end of December, recorded slower growth of 2.0% q-o-q in Q4 2024 versus 2.3% q-o-q in Q3 2024, amid reduced issuance during the quarter. In contrast, the corporate bond segment posted a 3.4% q-o-q expansion in Q4 2024, reversing the 1.7% q-o-q contraction in the prior quarter, buoyed by robust issuance. Meanwhile, the stock of central bank securities was only marginally changed in Q4 2024 on growth of 0.3% q-o-q.

Figure 2: Composition of Local Currency Bonds Outstanding in Indonesia

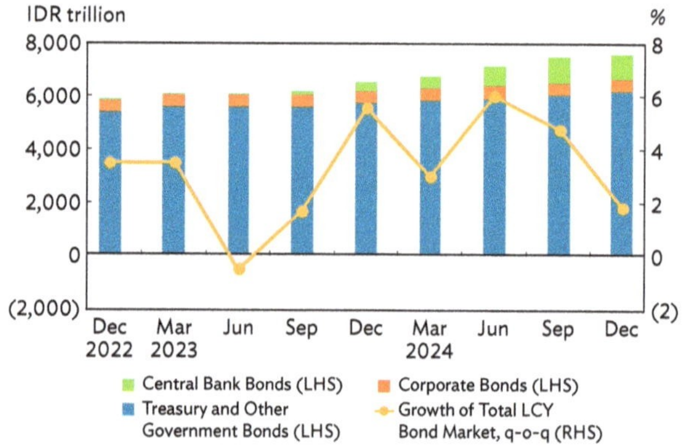

( ) = negative, IDR = Indonesian rupiah, LCY = local currency, LHS = left-hand side, q-o-q = quarter-on-quarter, RHS = right-hand side.

Notes: Data include *sukuk* (Islamic bonds). Data for Treasury and other government bonds comprise tradable and nontradable central government bonds.

Sources: Bank Indonesia; Directorate General of Budget Financing and Risk Management, Ministry of Finance; and Indonesia Stock Exchange.

In Q4 2024, LCY bond issuance fell 10.5% q-o-q to IDR693.5 trillion due to reduced issuance by the government. Treasury bond issuance declined 22.9% q-o-q in Q4 2024 as the government had already front-loaded issuance earlier in the year (**Figure 3**). On the other hand, corporate bond issuance posted strong growth of 62.2% q-o-q, buoyed by lower borrowing costs following the policy rate cut in September as well as refinancing needs of some companies due to bond maturities. The largest corporate bond issuance during the quarter came from Indah Kiat Pulp & Paper, which raised an aggregate IDR8.3 trillion via multiple tranches of conventional bonds and *sukuk* (Islamic bonds), accounting for 16.3% of the Q4 2024 corporate issuance total.

This market summary was written by Roselyn Regalado, consultant, Economic Research and Development Impact Department, Asian Development Bank, Manila.

Figure 3: Composition of Local Currency Bond Issuance in Indonesia

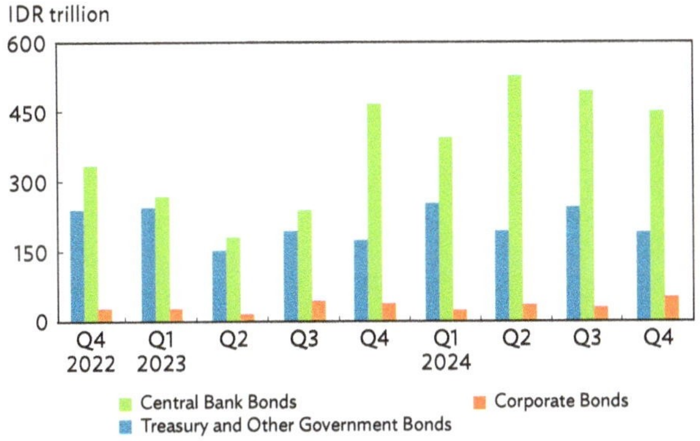

IDR = Indonesian rupiah, Q1 = first quarter, Q2 = second quarter, Q3 = third quarter, Q4 = fourth quarter.

Notes: Data include *sukuk* (Islamic bonds). Data for Treasury and other government bonds comprise tradable and nontradable central government bonds.

Sources: Bank Indonesia; Directorate General of Budget Financing and Risk Management, Ministry of Finance; and Indonesia Stock Exchange.

Investor Profile

Indonesia continued to have the most diverse investor ownership structure among all LCY bond markets in emerging East Asia.[14] At the end of December, domestic investors held 85.5% of tradable sovereign bonds, while foreign investors accounted for a 14.5% share. Among domestic investors, the largest holder was the central bank with an overall holdings share of 26.8% at the end of December. Central bank holdings comprised a significant 29.6% of the conventional bond stock, compared with only a 14.8% share of all *sukuk* holdings (**Figure 4**). Since 2020, Bank Indonesia has ramped up its holdings of government bonds as part of its monetary operations. Institutional investors such as banks and insurance and pension funds, which typically account for the largest bond holdings share among emerging East Asian peers, accounted for a much smaller holdings share of only 17.4% and 19.0%, respectively, in Indonesia. Within the region, Indonesia had the most diversified investor base, reflected by its low Herfindahl–Hirschman Index score.[15]

Sustainable Bond Market

At the end of December, Indonesia's sustainable bond market comprised predominantly green bond instruments, public sector issuances, and bonds denominated in foreign currency. The outstanding size of sustainable bonds tallied USD13.9 billion, with growth decelerating to 1.8% q-o-q in Q4 2024 from 10.2% q-o-q in Q3 2024, driven in part by a contraction in issuance. Green bonds were still the prevalent bond type, accounting for 73.8% of the outstanding sustainable bond stock at the end of December, followed by sustainability bonds at a smaller share of 20.8% (**Figure 5**). The public sector is an active issuer of sustainable bonds, accounting for 65.4% of the sustainable bond stock. This contributes to the longer maturity profile in Indonesia and an average size-weighted tenor of 8.1 years. Similar with other emerging East Asian markets, sustainable bond financing in Indonesia was mostly denominated in foreign currency (68.6%).

Figure 4: Investor Profile of Tradable Central Government Bonds

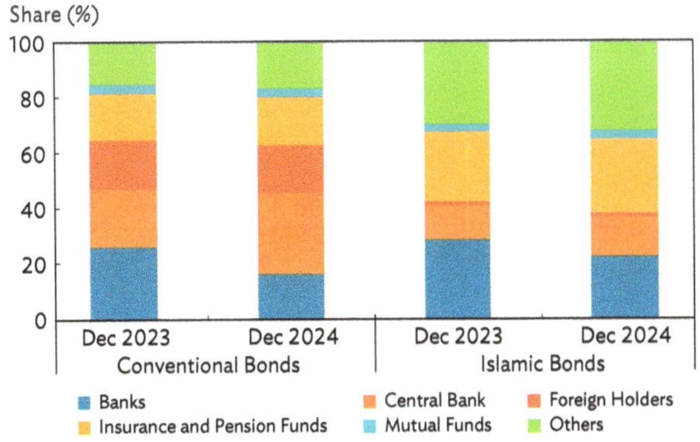

Source: Directorate General of Budget Financing and Risk Management, Ministry of Finance.

Figure 5: Market Profile of Outstanding Sustainable Bonds in Indonesia at the End of December 2024

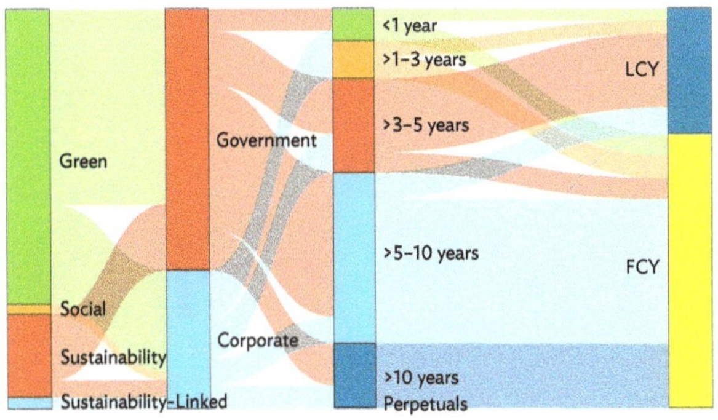

FCY = foreign currency, LCY = local currency.

Source: *AsianBondsOnline* calculations based on Bloomberg LP data.

[14] Emerging East Asia is defined to include member states of the Association of Southeast Asian Nations plus the People's Republic of China; Hong Kong, China; and the Republic of Korea.

[15] The Herfindahl–Hirschman Index is a common measure of market concentration. The index is used to measure the investor profile diversification of the local currency bond market by summing the squared share of each investor group in the bond market.

Republic of Korea

Yield Movements

Local currency (LCY) government bond yields in the Republic of Korea fell for all tenors between 1 December 2024 and 28 February 2025. Yields fell an average of 11 basis points (bps) across all tenors, with tenors of 1 year and below declining the most at an average of 21 bps (**Figure 1**). Yields fell on increased expectations of further rate cuts by the Bank of Korea as economic growth is expected to slow in 2025. The Bank of Korea, in its 25 February monetary policy meeting, cut the base rate by 25 bps to 2.75% to support the economy and mitigate downside risks to growth. These include developments in both trade policies in the United States and the domestic political situation. The Bank of Korea also lowered its 2025 annual growth forecast to 1.5% from the November forecast of 1.9%, while the inflation forecast was maintained at 1.9%. The Republic of Korea's economic growth slowed to 1.2% year-on-year in the fourth quarter (Q4) of 2024 from 1.5% year-on-year in the third quarter due to weaker consumer spending and export growth, and a continued contraction in investments.

Figure 1: The Republic of Korea's Benchmark Yield Curve—Local Currency Government Bonds

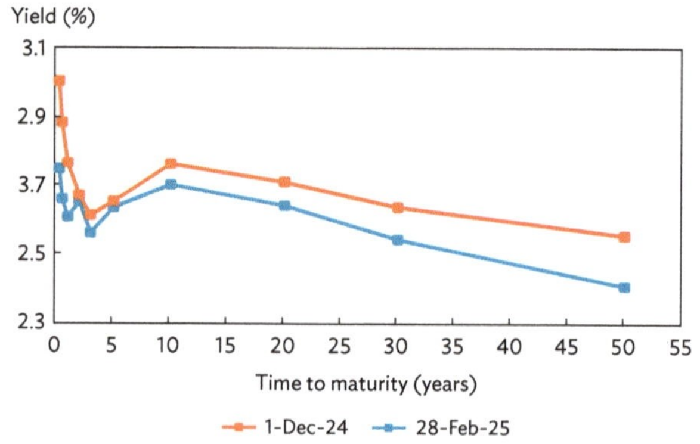

Source: Based on data from Bloomberg LP.

Figure 2: Composition of Local Currency Bonds Outstanding in the Republic of Korea

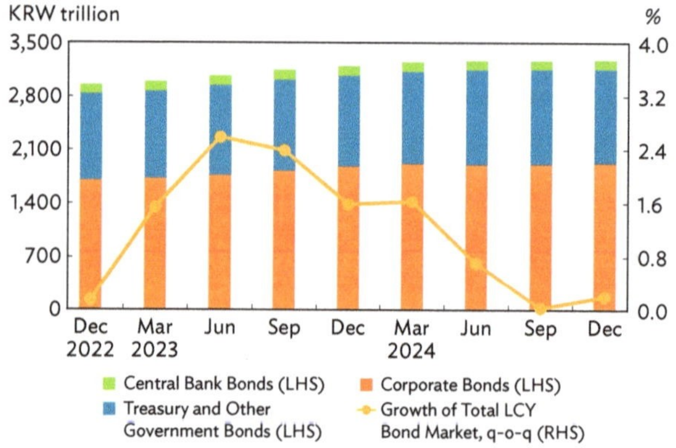

KRW = Korean won, LCY = local currency, LHS = left-hand side, q-o-q = quarter-on-quarter, RHS = right-hand side.

Sources: Bank of Korea and KG Zeroin Corp.

Local Currency Bond Market Size and Issuance

The size of the Republic of Korea's LCY bond market posted minimal growth of 0.2% quarter-on-quarter (q-o-q) in Q4 2024, driven by the corporate bond market. The Republic of Korea continued to be the second-largest LCY bond market in emerging East Asia with a size of KRW3,298.5 trillion at the end of December, accounting for 8.5% of the total regional bond market.[16] Corporate bonds continued to comprise a majority of the Republic of Korea's LCY bond market in Q4 2024 with a share of 58.7% (**Figure 2**). The stock of corporate bonds grew 0.6% q-o-q in Q4 2024, supported by a surge in issuance during the quarter. Government bonds, with a share of 37.8% of the total LCY bond market, fell 0.5% q-o-q on reduced borrowing.

LCY bond issuance rose 18.0% q-o-q to KRW284.9 trillion in Q4 2024 as the issuance of corporate bonds surged during the quarter. Issuance of corporate bonds rose 35.8% q-o-q in Q4 2024, versus 7.4% q-o-q in the previous quarter, as companies continued to take advantage of declining bond yields amid market expectations of rate cuts by the Bank of Korea

This market summary was written by Angelica Andrea Cruz, consultant, Economic Research and Development Impact Department, Asian Development Bank, Manila.

16 Emerging East Asia is defined to include member states of the Association of Southeast Asian Nations plus the People's Republic of China; Hong Kong, China; and the Republic of Korea.

Figure 3: Composition of Local Currency Bond Issuance in the Republic of Korea

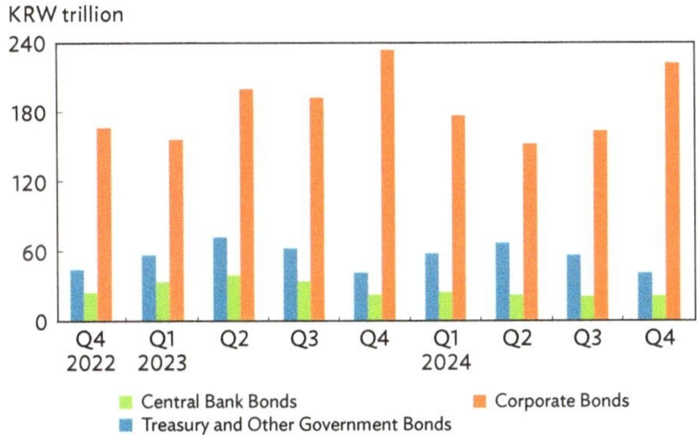

KRW = Korean won, Q1 = first quarter, Q2 = second quarter, Q3 = third quarter, Q4 = fourth quarter.

Sources: Bank of Korea and KG Zeroin Corp.

Figure 4: Local Currency Bonds Outstanding Investor Profile

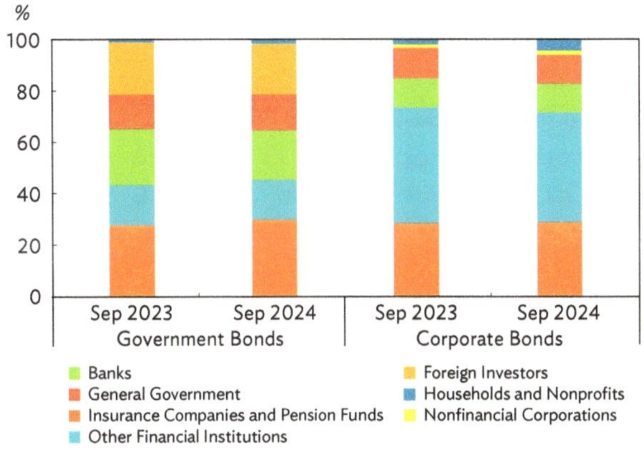

Sources: *AsianBondsOnline* and Bank of Korea.

(**Figure 3**). Meanwhile, issuance of government bonds contracted 27.6% q-o-q in Q4 2024 as the government had already fulfilled most of its borrowing requirements in previous quarters.

Investor Profile

Insurance companies and pension funds remained the largest investor group in the Republic of Korea's LCY bond market at the end of September. The Republic of Korea's LCY government bond market continued to have one of the most diverse investor bases in emerging East Asia as almost all outstanding bonds are held by five major investor groups. Insurance companies and pension funds had the largest share of LCY government bond holdings at 30.0%, followed by foreign investors and banks at 19.6% and 19.2%, respectively (**Figure 4**). Other major investor groups include other financial institutions (15.5%) and the general government (14.1%). On the other hand, the Republic of Korea's LCY corporate bond market still largely comprises two major investor groups: other financial institutions (42.7%) and insurance companies and pension funds (29.0%).

Sustainable Bond Market

Social bonds continued to dominate the Republic of Korea's sustainable bond market at the end of December 2024. The size of the Republic of Korea's sustainable bond market slightly rose 0.7% q-o-q to USD184.2 billion, making it the second-largest sustainable bond market in emerging East Asia at the end of December. The government and private sector are both active issuers of sustainable bonds with almost equal shares of outstanding sustainable bonds at 46.5% and 53.5%, respectively. Social bonds comprised 53.1% of the sustainable bond market and were largely issued by the government (**Figure 5**). Meanwhile, green bonds accounted for 29.5% and largely came from the private sector. The remaining maturities of outstanding sustainable bonds remained concentrated in tenors of less than 3 years (66.3%), resulting in a size-weighted average tenor of 3.0 years. In terms of currency denomination, nearly 60% of outstanding sustainable bonds at the end of December were denominated in Korean won.

Figure 5: Market Profile of Outstanding Sustainable Bonds in the Republic of Korea at the End of December 2024

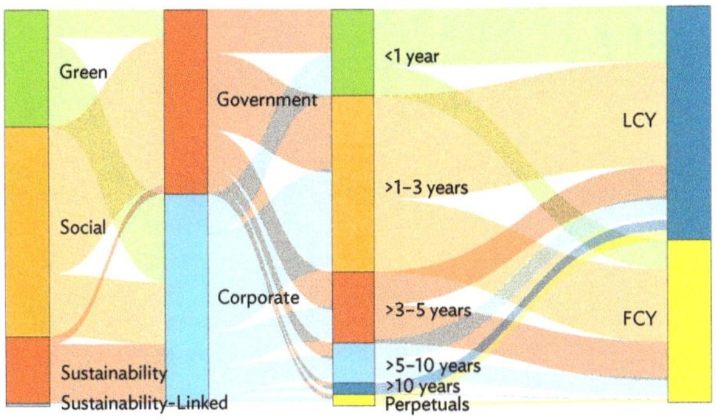

FCY = foreign currency, LCY = local currency.

Source: *AsianBondsOnline* calculations based on Bloomberg LP data.

Lao People's Democratic Republic

Size and Composition

The Lao People's Democratic Republic's (Lao PDR) bond market reached a size of USD4.1 billion at the end of 2023, growing 4.8% year-on-year (y-o-y) from USD3.9 billion in 2022. The Lao PDR's bond market as a share of gross domestic product (GDP) stabilized at around 32.0% at the end of 2023 from 33.6% a year earlier (**Figure 1**). With the government's continued efforts to further develop the local currency (LCY) bond market and reduce reliance on foreign currency (FCY) financing, available data show that the share of LCY bonds to total bonds increased to 36.0% in 2023 from 31.1% in 2022—while nearly tripling from 12.7% in 2018 (**Figure 2**).[17] Meanwhile, the share of FCY bonds declined to 64.0% of the total in 2023 from 68.9% in 2022.

Continuing last year's momentum, onshore bond issuance through the Lao Securities Exchange (LSX) increased significantly in 2023. Total bond issuance through the LSX rose 144.3% y-o-y to USD199.8 million in 2023—nearly all of which was government issuance—from USD81.8 million in 2022. In 2023, the Government of the Lao PDR issued bonds denominated in both Lao kip and foreign currencies via the LSX to support cash flow management and strengthen debt management. Issuance of LCY government bonds surged 166.1% y-o-y to LAK3.7 trillion (USD180.3 million) in 2023 from LAK1.4 trillion in 2022 (**Figure 3**). Meanwhile, issuance of FCY government bonds increased 17.5% y-o-y

Figure 1: Bond Markets as Share of Gross Domestic Product in Select Members of the Association of Southeast Asian Nations

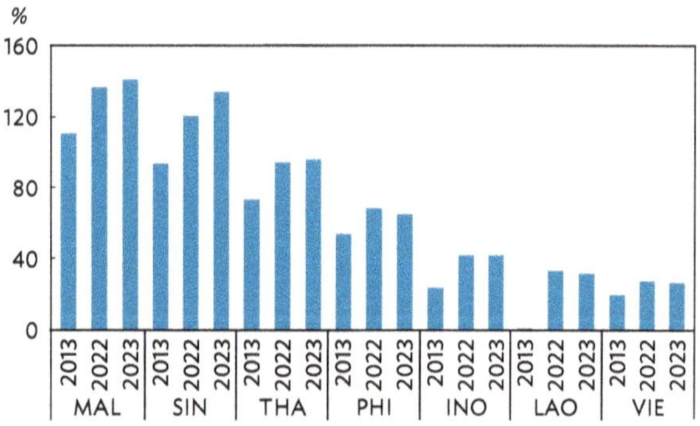

INO = Indonesia, LAO = Lao People's Democratic Republic, MAL = Malaysia, PHI = Philippines, SIN = Singapore, THA = Thailand, VIE = Viet Nam.

Note: Data for gross domestic product are from CEIC Data Company.

Source: *AsianBondsOnline* calculations based on various sources.

Figure 2: Composition of Total Bonds Outstanding in the Lao People's Democratic Republic

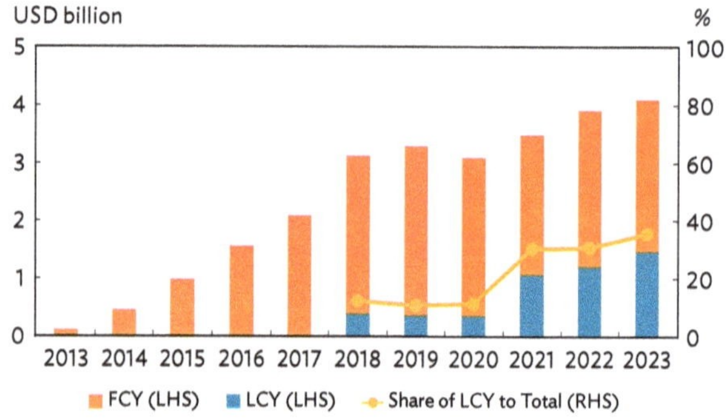

FCY = foreign currency, LCY = local currency, LHS = left-hand side, RHS = right-hand side, USD = United States dollar.

Notes:

1. FCY data include bonds issued in the Lao Securities Exchange, Singapore Exchange, and the Thai Bond Market Association.
2. Figures computed based on 31 December 2023 currency exchange rates to remove currency effects.

Sources: Lao Securities Exchange, Ministry of Finance Lao PDR, Singapore Exchange, and Thai Bond Market Association.

Figure 3: Government Bonds Issued Through the Lao Securities Exchange

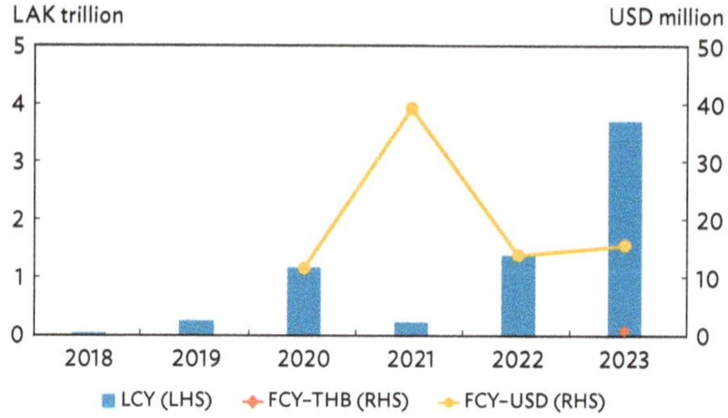

FCY = foreign currency, LAK = Lao kip, LCY = local currency, LHS = left-hand side, RHS = right-hand side, THB = Thai baht, USD = United States dollar.

Source: Lao Securities Exchange.

This market summary was written by Angelica Andrea Cruz, consultant, Economic Research and Development Impact Department, Asian Development Bank, Manila.

17 LCY bonds are bonds denominated in Lao kip, while foreign currency bonds are denominated in currencies other than Lao kip. Definitions do not take into account where the bonds were issued (i.e., onshore or offshore).

to USD16.5 million in 2023—most of which were denominated in US dollars—from USD14.0 million in 2022. In September 2023, the government issued its first THB-denominated bonds through the LSX, financing THB28.8 million (USD0.8 million). The LSX witnessed its first corporate bond issuance in June 2023 as Souvanny Home Center raised USD3.0 million worth of USD-denominated bonds.

Local Currency Bond Market Size and Issuance

LCY bonds outstanding increased 21.2% y-o-y to LAK30.6 trillion at the end of 2023 from LAK25.3 trillion a year earlier, driven by the issuance of triangular bonds and fiscal deficit financing bonds.[18] All LCY bonds outstanding at the end of 2023 were government-issued. Triangular bonds outstanding increased 65.4% y-o-y to LAK9.1 trillion at the end of December from LAK5.5 trillion a year earlier, while fiscal deficit financing bonds increased 43.9% y-o-y to LAK4.1 trillion from LAK2.8 trillion during the same period. At the end of 2023, recapitalization bonds and triangular bonds collectively comprised over 60% of the Lao PDR's LCY bond market. Specifically, recapitalization bonds (LAK10.2 trillion) accounted for one-third of total LCY bonds outstanding at the end of December 2023, followed by triangular bonds (29.7%, LAK9.1 trillion), investment bonds (17.8%, LAK5.5 trillion), fiscal deficit financing bonds issued via the LSX (13.3%, LAK4.1 trillion), and Treasury bills (5.9%, LAK1.8 trillion) (**Figure 4**).

The remaining average maturity of outstanding LCY bonds listed on the LSX in 2023 were mostly short-term, though the market's average remaining tenor has improved since 2022. At the end of 2023, nearly all (99.4%) LCY bonds outstanding had remaining tenors of more than 1 year to 3 years (**Figure 5**). The average size-weighted tenor of LCY bonds outstanding was 1.0 years in 2023, up from 0.6 years in 2022.

Total onshore LCY bond issuance rose 49.1% y-o-y to LAK9.8 trillion in 2023 from LAK6.6 trillion in 2022. All LCY bond issuance in the Lao PDR bond market in 2023 came from the government, while the 49.1% y-o-y increase was largely driven by triangular bond issuance totaling LAK4.1 trillion during the year (**Figure 6**). Issuance of fiscal deficit financing bonds surged 166.1% y-o-y in 2023 to LAK3.7 trillion from LAK1.4 trillion in 2022. Treasury bill issuance also increased 68.6% y-o-y to LAK1.8 trillion from LAK1.1 trillion during the same period. Meanwhile, issuance of recapitalization bonds contracted 93.9% y-o-y to LAK0.3 trillion in 2023 from LAK4.1 trillion in 2022.

Figure 4: Composition of Local Currency Bonds Outstanding in the Lao People's Democratic Republic

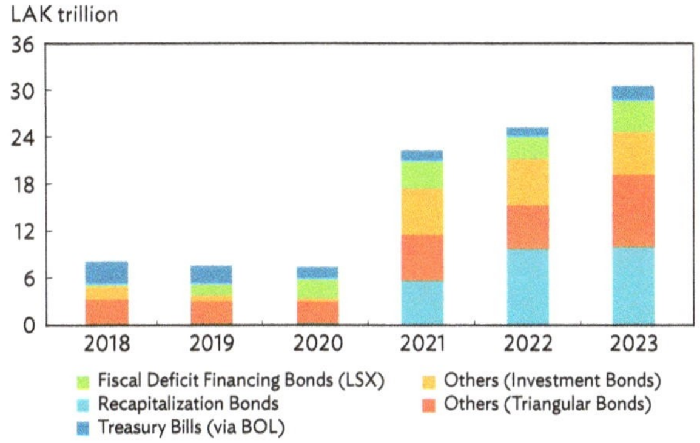

BOL = Bank of the Lao People's Democratic Republic, LAK = Lao kip, LSX = Lao Securities Exchange.

Note: There are no available data for local currency corporate bonds.

Source: Ministry of Finance Lao People's Democratic Republic.

Figure 5: Maturity Structure of Local Currency Bonds Outstanding Issued Through the Lao Securities Exchange

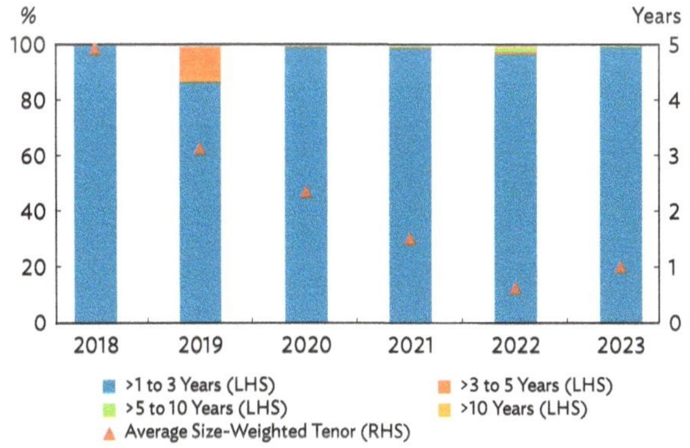

LHS = left-hand side, RHS = right-hand side.

Note: Data only include government bonds as there are no local currency corporate bonds issued through the Lao Securities Exchange.

Source: Lao Securities Exchange.

[18] Triangular bonds are Lao kip-denominated bonds issued for the repayment of expenditure arrears on completed public investment projects. Ministry of Finance, Government of the Lao PDR. 2023. Public and Publicly Guaranteed Debt Statistic Bulletin. Vientiane.

Figure 6: Local Currency Bond Issuance in the Lao People's Democratic Republic

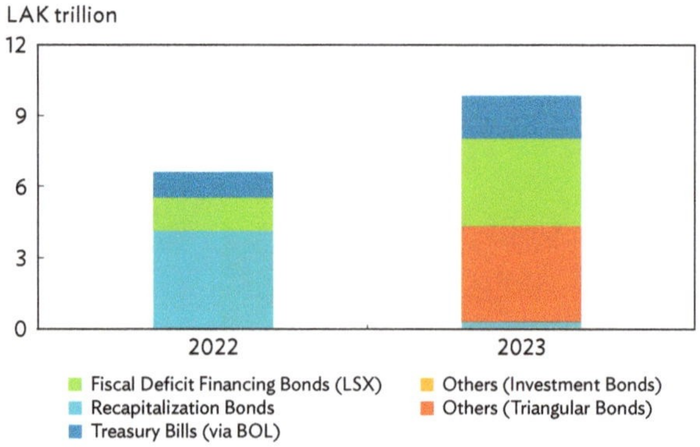

BOL = Bank of the Lao People's Democratic Republic, LAK = Lao kip, LSX = Lao Securities Exchange.

Note: There are no available data for LCY corporate bonds.

Source: Ministry of Finance Lao PDR.

Figure 7: Maturity Structure of Local Currency Bonds Issued Through the Lao Securities Exchange

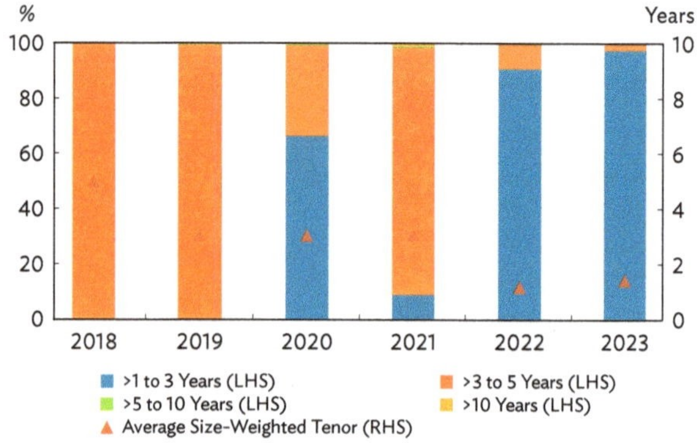

LHS = left-hand side, RHS = right-hand side.

Note: There is no local currency corporate bond issuance via the Lao Securities Exchange.

Source: Lao Securities Exchange.

LCY government bond issuance through the LSX in 2023 mainly comprised short-term tenors. In 2023, 97.4% of total LCY bonds issued through the LSX had tenors of more than 1 year to 3 years, while the remaining 2.6% had tenors of more than 3 years to 5 years (**Figure 7**). The average size-weighted tenor of LCY bond issuance in 2023 was 1.4 years, up slightly from 1.2 years in 2022 but still below the average for 2019–2021 of 3.1 years.

Foreign Currency Bond Market Size and Issuance

Total FCY bonds outstanding reached USD2.6 billion at the end of 2023, slightly down from USD2.7 billion a year earlier. The Lao PDR continued to have the second-highest FCY-bonds-to-GDP share among all members of the Association of Southeast Asian Nations at 20.5% (**Figure 8**). The Thai baht remained the predominant currency in the Lao PDR's FCY bond market, with THB-denominated bonds comprising 80.5% of total FCY bonds outstanding at the end of 2023 (**Figure 9**). FCY government bonds outstanding declined 6.7% y-o-y to USD1.1 billion at the end of 2023 from USD1.2 billion in 2022. The annual decline was primarily driven by reduced issuance and a large volume of maturities of FCY government bonds, resulting in a lower corresponding share of FCY government bonds to total FCY bonds of 40.5% in 2023 versus 42.2% in 2022. Meanwhile, FCY corporate bonds outstanding

Figure 8: Foreign Currency Bonds Outstanding as a Share of Gross Domestic Product in Select Members of the Association of Southeast Asian Nations

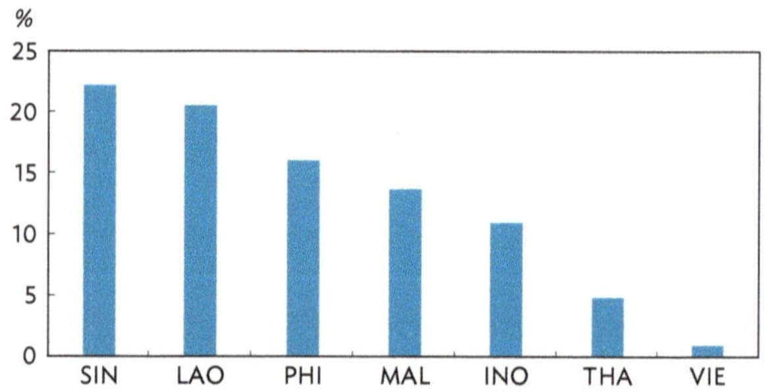

INO = Indonesia, LAO = Lao People's Democratic Republic, MAL = Malaysia, PHI = Philippines, SIN = Singapore, THA = Thailand, VIE = Viet Nam.

Notes: All data as of end-December 2023. Data for gross domestic product are from CEIC Data Company.

Source: *AsianBondsOnline* calculations based on various sources.

(USD1.6 billion) comprised 59.5% of total FCY bonds outstanding at the end of 2023 on marginal growth of 0.3% y-o-y.

The average remaining maturity of outstanding FCY bonds in the Lao PDR market was less than 5.0 years at the end of 2023. At the end of December 2023, nearly half of total FCY bonds outstanding had remaining tenors of more than 1 year to 3 years, 33.5% had tenors of more than 3 years to 5 years, and 21.2% had tenors of more than 5 years to 10 years (**Figure 10**). The average size-weighted tenor of FCY bonds outstanding was 4.6 years in 2023, up slightly from 4.0 years in 2022. The average

Figure 9: Composition of Foreign Currency Bonds Outstanding in the Lao People's Democratic Republic

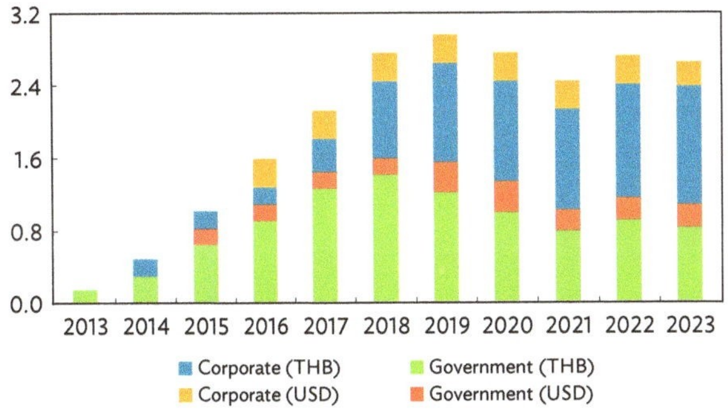

THB = Thai baht, USD = United States dollar.

Note: Figures computed based on 31 December 2023 exchange rates to remove currency effects.

Sources: Lao Securities Exchange, Singapore Exchange, and Thai Bond Market Association.

Figure 11: Composition of Foreign Currency Bond Issuance in the Lao People's Democratic Republic

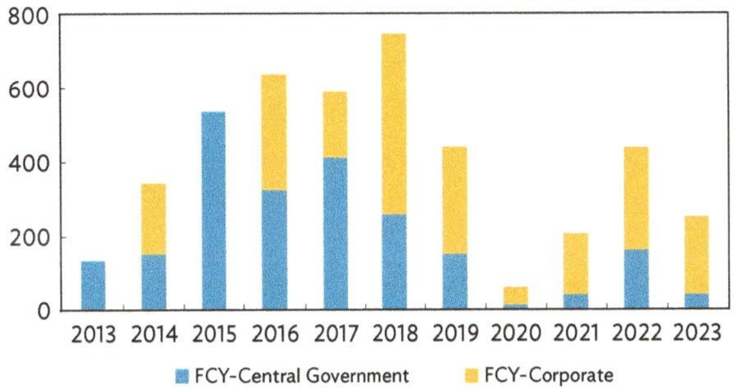

FCY = foreign currency, USD = United States dollar.

Note: Figures computed based on 31 December 2023 exchange rates to remove currency effects.

Sources: Lao Securities Exchange, Singapore Exchange, and Thai Bond Market Association.

Figure 10: Maturity Structure of Foreign Currency Bonds Outstanding Issued in the Lao People's Democratic Republic

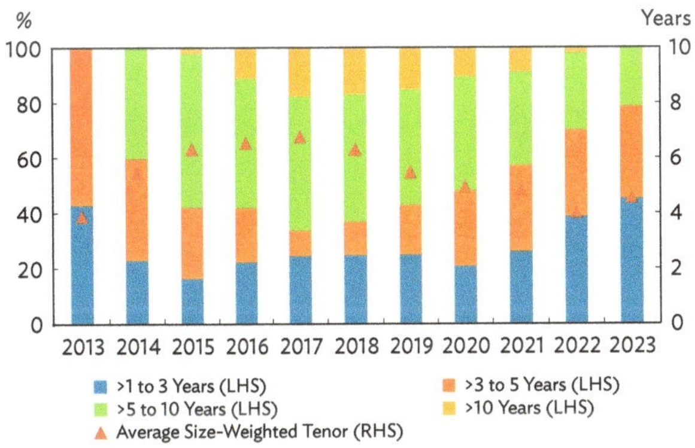

LHS = left-hand side, RHS = right-hand side.

Note: Figures were computed based on 31 December 2023 exchange rates to remove currency effects.

Sources: Lao Securities Exchange, Singapore Exchange, and Thai Bond Market Association.

Figure 12: Maturity Structure of Foreign Currency Government Bonds Issued Through the Lao Securities Exchange

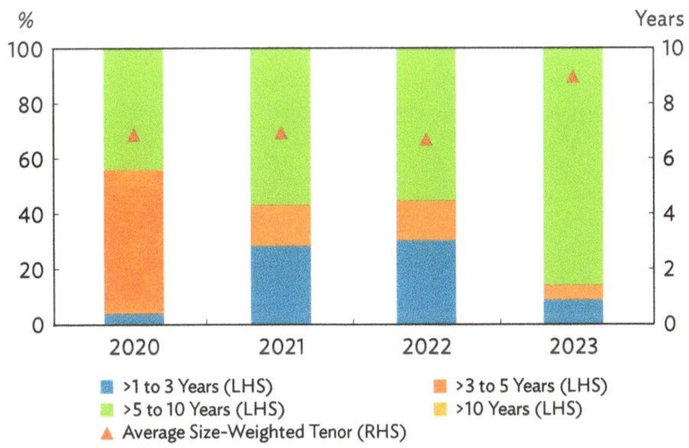

LHS = left-hand side, RHS = right-hand side.

Notes: All bonds issued in 2020–2022 were denominated in United States (US) dollars. Bonds issued in 2023 were denominated in US dollars and Thai baht.

Source: Lao Securities Exchange.

has remained below 5.0 years since 2020, which will have implications for refinancing needs in the coming years.

Total onshore government FCY issuance increased 17.5% y-o-y in 2023, and the average tenor length also increased compared with 2022. The Lao PDR's total FCY bond issuance, including both onshore and offshore issuance, declined sharply by 42.6% y-o-y to USD249.8 million in 2023 from USD434.9 million in 2022 (**Figure 11**). The higher-interest-rate environment and the depreciation of the Lao kip against the US dollar discouraged FCY bond issuance. However, the Government of the Lao PDR was able to issue more FCY bonds onshore through the LSX in 2023. The government issued USD16.5 million of FCY bonds via the LSX in 2023, up 17.5% y-o-y from USD14.0 million in 2022. These bonds were denominated in either Thai baht or US dollars, with tenors ranging from 1 year to 10 years and coupon rates of 5.0%–8.0%. The average size-weighted tenor of government FCY issuances via the LSX was 9.0 years in 2023, compared with 6.7 years in 2022 (**Figure 12**). Meanwhile, the first FCY corporate bond issuance onshore via the LSX was the USD3.0 million 4-year bond issued by Souvanny Home Center in June 2023.

Malaysia

Yield Movements

Between 1 December 2024 and 28 February 2025, local currency (LCY) government bond yields in Malaysia were broadly unchanged. Yields moved an average of less than 1 basis point across the curve on expectations that Bank Negara Malaysia would keep its monetary policy stance unchanged (**Figure 1**). On 6 March, Bank Negara Malaysia maintained the overnight policy rate at 3.00%, where it has remained since May 2023, amid a favorable economic performance and a moderating inflation outlook for 2025. Gross domestic product growth climbed to 5.1% year-on-year (y-o-y) in 2024 from 3.6% y-o-y in 2023, supported by strong investments and increased private consumption. Consumer price inflation moderated to 1.7% y-o-y in both January and December from 1.8% y-o-y in November.

Figure 1: Malaysia's Benchmark Yield Curve—Local Currency Government Bonds

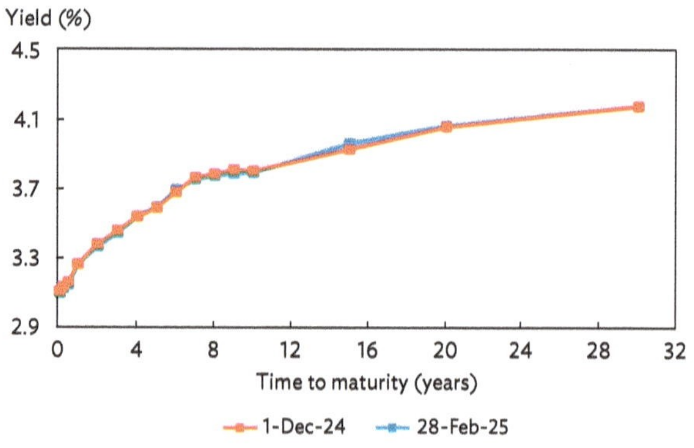

Source: Based on data from Bloomberg LP.

Local Currency Bond Market Size and Issuance

The LCY bond market of Malaysia reached a size of MYR2.1 trillion at the end of December, with growth easing to 0.8% quarter-on-quarter (q-o-q) in the fourth quarter (Q4) of 2024 from 0.9% in the third quarter (Q3). Government bond market growth moderated to 0.6% q-o-q in Q4 2024, from the previous quarter's 1.2% q-o-q, on reduced issuance and maturities during the quarter. Malaysia's corporate bond segment expanded 1.0% q-o-q in Q4 2024 despite a contraction in issuance due to reduced maturities during the quarter. At the end of December, there were no outstanding central bank bills as the central bank has not issued new securities since Q3 2024 (**Figure 2**). *Sukuk* (Islamic bonds) comprised a majority (63.2%) of the LCY bond market at the end of December.

Figure 2: Composition of Local Currency Bonds Outstanding in Malaysia

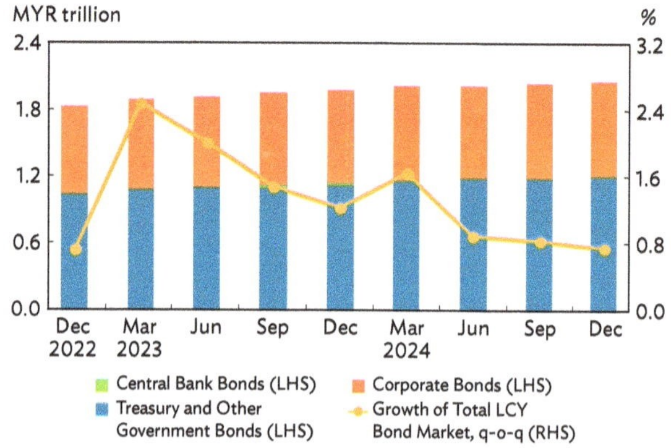

LCY = local currency, LHS = left-hand side, MYR = Malaysian ringgit, q-o-q = quarter-on-quarter, RHS = right-hand side.
Source: Bank Negara Malaysia Fully Automated System for Issuing/Tendering.

LCY bond issuance fell 23.5% q-o-q to MYR80.4 billion in Q4 2024 as government issuance contracted. Government bond issuance declined 43.4% q-o-q in Q4 2024 as the Government of Malaysia front-loaded annual issuance in the prior quarters (**Figure 3**). Meanwhile, corporate bond issuance decreased 1.2% q-o-q in Q4 2024, reversing the growth of 18.2% q-o-q in Q3 2024. Cagamas was the largest issuer of LCY bonds in Q4 2024 as it issued conventional and *sukuk* commercial paper and medium-term notes totaling MYR5.3 billion, which accounted for 6.6% of total LCY bond issuance in Q4 2024.

This market summary was written by Justin Adrian Villas, consultant, Economic Research and Development Impact Department, Asian Development Bank, Manila.

Figure 3: Composition of Local Currency Bond Issuance in Malaysia

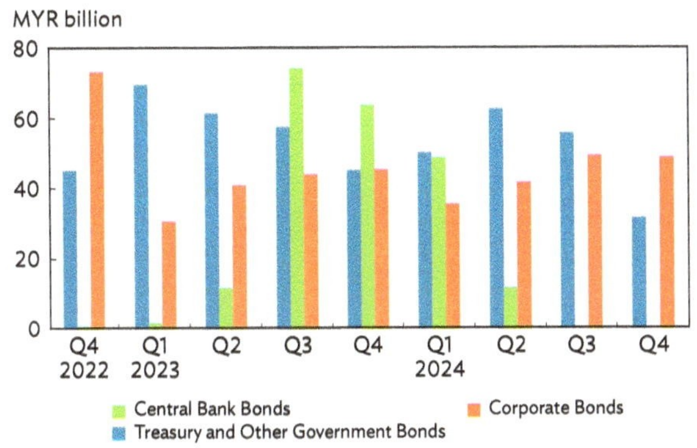

MYR = Malaysian ringgit, Q1 = first quarter, Q2 = second quarter, Q3 = third quarter, Q4 = fourth quarter.

Source: Bank Negara Malaysia Fully Automated System for Issuing/Tendering.

Investor Profile

At the end of September, domestic investors held 77.6% of all Malaysian LCY government bonds outstanding. Financial institutions and social security institutions accounted for the largest holdings shares at 31.6% and 29.7%, respectively (**Figure 4**). The share of foreign holdings in the Malaysian government bond market was 22.4% at the end of September, the largest among its emerging East Asian peers.[19]

Figure 4: Local Currency Government Bonds Investor Profile

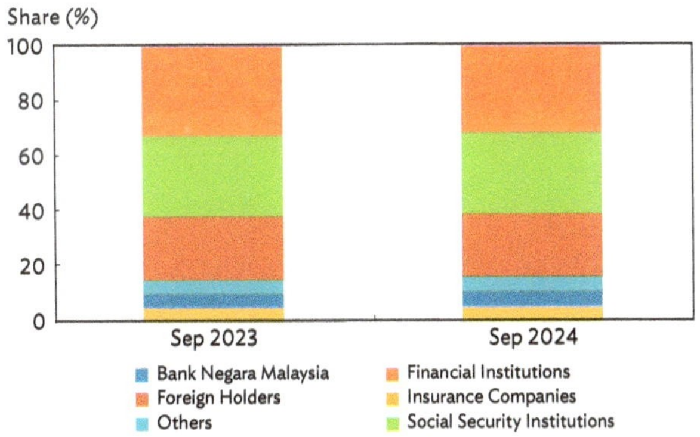

Note: "Others" include statutory bodies, nominees and trustee companies, and cooperatives and unclassified items.

Source: Bank Negara Malaysia.

Sustainable Bond Market

At the end of December, long-term corporate bonds comprised most of Malaysia's sustainable bond market. The total sustainable debt stock decreased to a size of USD15.4 billion at the end of December on a 0.1% q-o-q contraction in Q4 2024, with most bonds denominated in Malaysian ringgit (88.0%). The majority of sustainable bonds outstanding comprised sustainability bonds (70.8%), while green bonds accounted for a 19.0% share (**Figure 5**). Corporate bonds dominate the sustainable bond market, making up 77.2% of the total stock at the end of December, with 59.7% of outstanding corporate bonds carrying tenors of more than 5 years. Outstanding sustainable bonds from the public sector, which comprised 22.8% of the total, carried maturities of over 5 years. At the end of December, the size-weighted average tenor of outstanding sustainable bonds in Malaysia was 8.8 years.

Figure 5: Market Profile of Outstanding Sustainable Bonds in Malaysia at the End of December 2024

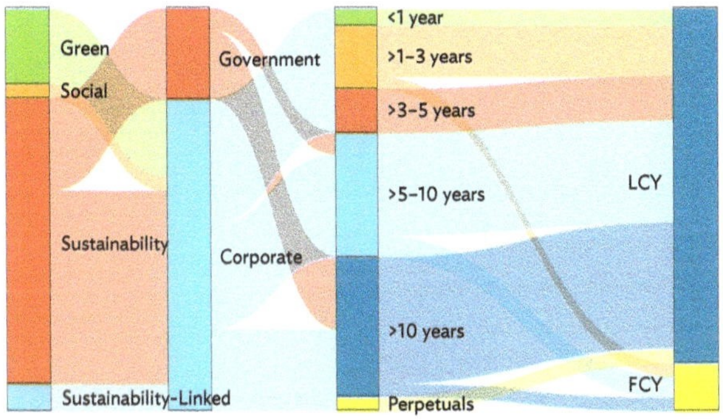

FCY = foreign currency, LCY = local currency.

Source: *AsianBondsOnline* calculations based on Bloomberg LP data.

[19] Emerging East Asia is defined to include member states of the Association of Southeast Asian Nations plus the People's Republic of China; Hong Kong, China; and the Republic of Korea.

Philippines

Yield Movements

Between 1 December 2024 and 28 February 2025, local currency (LCY) sovereign bond yields in the Philippines rose for longer tenors (Figure 1). Yields for maturities of 7 years and longer rose an average of 13 basis points (bps), as the Bangko Sentral ng Pilipinas (BSP) held its overnight reverse repurchase rate steady at 5.75% on 13 February due to uncertainties over global economic policies and their potential impact on the domestic economy. The rise in yields was also influenced by expectations of fewer rate cuts this year. BSP Governor Eli M. Remolona Jr., on 1 February, signaled total rate cuts of 50 bps in 2025, which was less than the 100 bps previously signaled by the BSP in November. In contrast, yields for tenors of 5 years or less—except for the 1-month tenor—fell an average of 17 bps amid subdued inflation and slow economic growth. The Philippine economy grew 5.6% in full-year 2024, falling short of the government's target range of 6.0%–6.5% growth due to weather disruptions, weak consumption, and geopolitical tensions. Meanwhile, year-on-year inflation slowed to 2.1% in February from 2.9% in January, driven by slower increases in food and beverage prices.

Figure 1: The Philippines' Benchmark Yield Curve—Local Currency Government Bonds

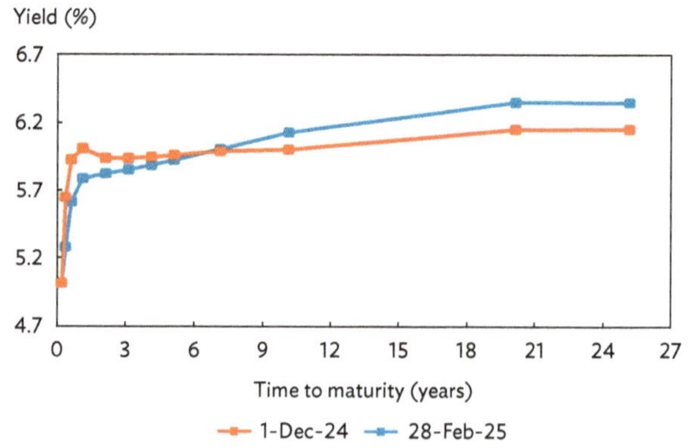

Source: Based on data from Bloomberg LP.

Local Currency Bond Market Size and Issuance

Contractions in the stock of government bonds and central bank securities dragged down the LCY bond market at the end of December. The total LCY debt stock contracted 0.6% quarter-on-quarter (q-o-q) in the fourth quarter (Q4) of 2024 to a size of PHP12.9 trillion (**Figure 2**). The decline was driven by reduced issuance from the government and the central bank during the quarter. Treasury and other government bonds recorded a slight dip of 0.1% q-o-q, while BSP securities were down 11.7% q-o-q. Conversely, despite a reduction in issuance, total corporate debt stock grew 2.6% q-o-q in Q4 2024 due to fewer maturities during the quarter.

Figure 2: Composition of Local Currency Bonds Outstanding in the Philippines

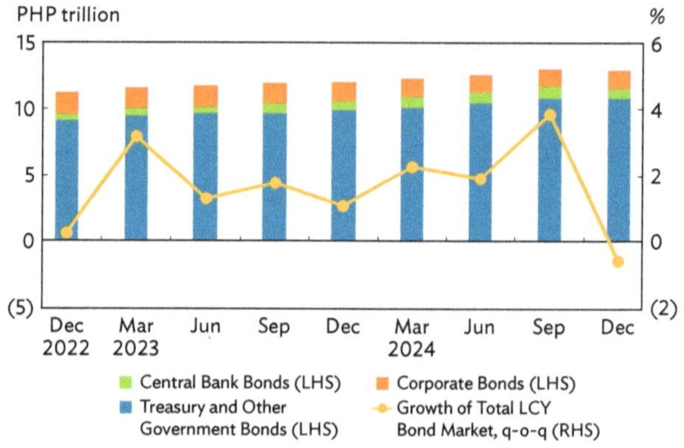

( ) = negative, LCY = local currency, LHS = left-hand side, PHP = Philippine peso, q-o-q = quarter-on-quarter, RHS = right-hand side.

Note: Treasury and other government bonds comprise Treasury bonds, Treasury bills, and bonds issued by government agencies, entities, and corporations for which repayment is guaranteed by the Government of the Philippines.

Sources: Bangko Sentral ng Pilipinas, Bureau of the Treasury, and Bloomberg LP.

LCY bond issuance contracted in Q4 2024 on reduced issuance for all bond segments. Total LCY bond issuance fell 19.2% q-o-q to PHP2.4 trillion in Q4 2024 (**Figure 3**). The issuance of Treasury and other government bonds declined 48.2% q-o-q due to the government's reduced borrowing after meeting its financing needs in the prior quarters. Similarly, total corporate bond issuance dropped 63.3% q-o-q in Q4 2024 largely due to the exceptionally high issuance volume in the previous quarter. The largest corporate bond issuance during the quarter came from SMC Tollways, with total debt sale of PHP35.0 billion, accounting for 57.7% of the Philippines' total LCY corporate bond issuance during the quarter. Additionally, in November, Ayala Land issued a 10-year sustainability-linked bond worth PHP8.0 billion.

This market summary was written by Jeremy Grace Ilustrisimo, consultant, Economic Research and Development Impact Department, Asian Development Bank, Manila.

Figure 3: Composition of Local Currency Bond Issuance in the Philippines

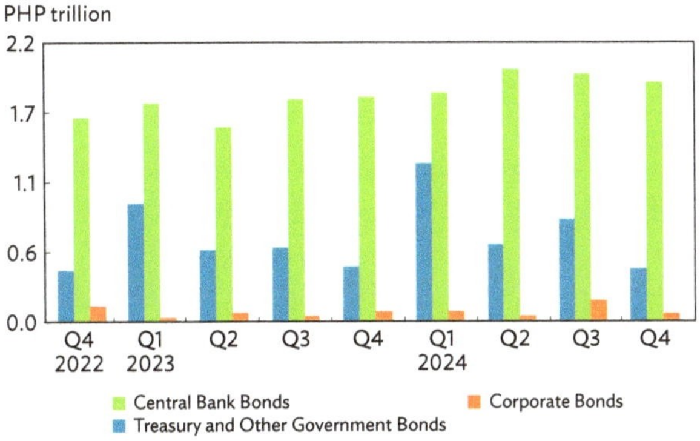

PHP = Philippine peso, Q1 = first quarter, Q2 = second quarter, Q3 = third quarter, Q4 = fourth quarter.

Note: Treasury and other government bonds comprise Treasury bonds, Treasury bills, and bonds issued by government agencies, entities, and corporations for which repayment is guaranteed by the Government of the Philippines.

Sources: Bangko Sentral ng Pilipinas, Bureau of the Treasury, and Bloomberg LP.

Figure 4: Investor Profile of Local Currency Government Bonds

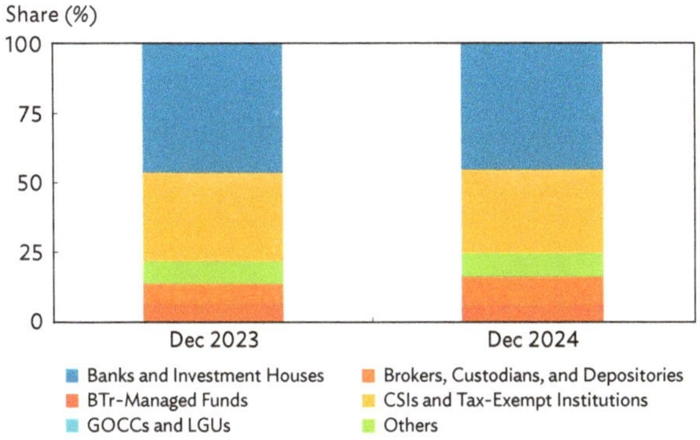

BTr = Bureau of the Treasury, CSI = contractual savings institution, GOCC = government-owned or -controlled corporation, LGU = local government unit.

Note: At the end of December, the aggregate holdings share for government-owned or -controlled corporations and local government units was 0.01%, amounting to PHP1.1 billion.

Source: Bureau of the Treasury.

Investor Profile

At the end of December, the investor base of the Philippines' LCY government bond market was among the least diverse in emerging East Asia.[20] The Philippines had the third-highest Herfindahl–Hirschman Index score in the region at the end of December.[21] This was because over 70.0% of the economy's LCY government debt stock was held by only two dominant investor groups: (i) banks and investment houses, and (ii) contractual savings institutions and tax-exempt institutions (**Figure 4**). Collectively, their holdings share accounted for 75.2% at the end of December, down from 78.1% a year earlier.

Figure 5: Market Profile of Outstanding Sustainable Bonds in the Philippines at the End of December 2024

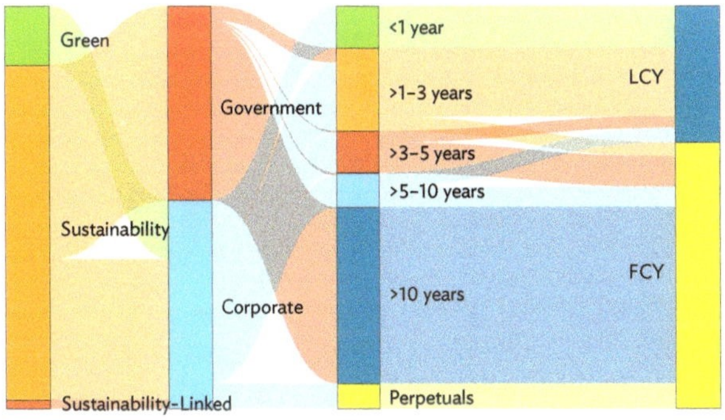

FCY = foreign currency, LCY = local currency.

Source: *AsianBondsOnline* calculations based on Bloomberg LP data.

Sustainable Bond Market

Foreign-currency-denominated sustainability bond instruments remained prevalent in the Philippines' sustainable bond market in Q4 2024. By the end of December, sustainability bonds accounted for 83.2% of the market's total sustainable debt stock, approximately 71.0% of which were denominated in a foreign currency (**Figure 5**). At the end of Q4 2024, total outstanding sustainable bonds grew 4.0% q-o-q to USD11.3 billion, with the public and private sectors each contributing a roughly equal share of the market. Over 90.0% of the public sector's sustainable bonds carried tenors of over 5 years, while the private sector's corresponding share was only 27.4%. Consequently, the size-weighted average tenor of the Philippines' sustainable bond market stood at 12.4 years at the end of December versus a size-weighted average of 4.5 years for ASEAN+3 economies.[22]

[20] Emerging East Asia is defined to include member states of the Association of Southeast Asian Nations plus the People's Republic of China; Hong Kong, China; and the Republic of Korea.

[21] The Herfindahl–Hirschman Index is a common measure of market concentration. The index is used to measure the investor profile diversification of the local currency bond market by summing the squared share of each investor group in the bond market.

[22] ASEAN+3 is defined to include member states of the Association of Southeast Asian Nations (ASEAN) plus the People's Republic of China; Hong Kong, China; Japan; and the Republic of Korea.

Singapore

Yield Movements

Between 1 December 2024 and 28 February 2025, local currency (LCY) government bond yields in Singapore fell for most securities. Bond yields fell an average of 16 basis points for tenors of 15 years or less (except for 1-year bonds) as the Monetary Authority of Singapore (MAS) eased its monetary policy stance amid slower inflation (**Figure 1**). On 24 January, the MAS reduced the slope of the Singapore dollar's nominal effective exchange rate, while retaining its width and the level at which it is centered, on anticipated slower growth and cooling inflation in 2025. Consumer price inflation slowed to 1.2% year-on-year in January 2025 from 1.5% in the previous month. On the other hand, yields rose an average of 5 basis points for long-term securities (20-year to 30-year bonds), tracking the movement in yields of Treasuries in the United States.

Figure 1: Singapore's Benchmark Yield Curve—Local Currency Government Bonds

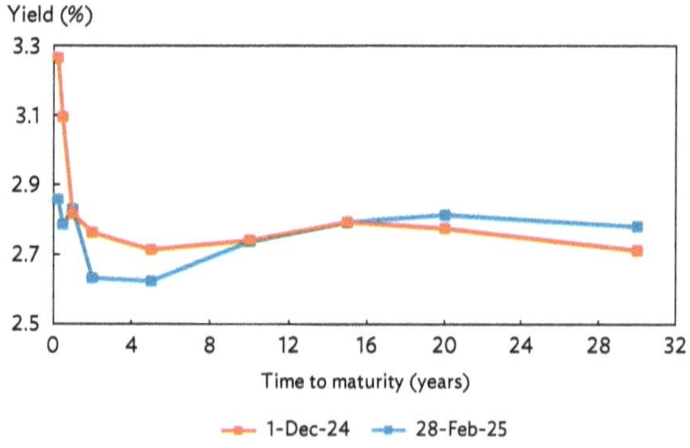

Source: Based on data from Bloomberg LP.

Local Currency Bond Market Size and Issuance

Singapore's LCY bond market reached a size of SGD849.6 billion at the end of December. Total LCY bond growth slowed to 1.6% quarter-on-quarter (q-o-q) in the fourth quarter (Q4) of 2024 from a 1.8% q-o-q expansion in the third quarter (Q3). Outstanding Treasuries posted faster growth of 1.4% q-o-q in Q4 2024, up from 0.6% q-o-q in the prior quarter, due to increased issuance of Treasury bills. On the other hand, central bank bills grew at a slower pace of 1.2% q-o-q, versus growth of 4.4% q-o-q in Q3 2024, due to increased maturities during Q4 2024 (**Figure 2**). Meanwhile, the corporate bond segment grew 2.5% q-o-q in Q4 2024, recovering from a contraction of 0.7% q-o-q in Q3 2024 amid increased issuance. At the end of December, the state-owned Housing & Development Board continued to have the largest amount of bonds outstanding in the LCY corporate bond market, amounting to SGD30.0 billion and comprising 14.8% of outstanding corporate bonds.

Figure 2: Composition of Local Currency Bonds Outstanding in Singapore

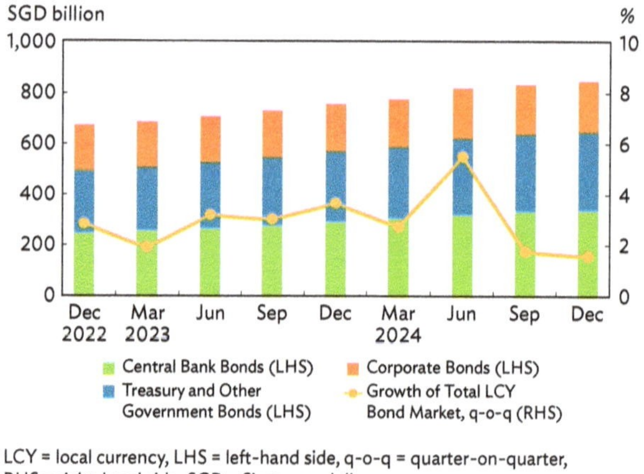

LCY = local currency, LHS = left-hand side, q-o-q = quarter-on-quarter, RHS = right-hand side, SGD = Singapore dollar.

Note: Corporate bonds are based on *AsianBondsOnline* estimates.

Sources: Monetary Authority of Singapore and Bloomberg LP.

This market summary was written by Justin Adrian Villas, consultant, Economic Research and Development Impact Department, Asian Development Bank, Manila.

LCY bond issuance posted growth of 3.0% q-o-q in Q4 2024, a reversal of the previous quarter's contraction of 3.7% q-o-q. Total issuance soared to SGD561.1 billion in Q4 2024, with all bond segments posting q-o-q increases. Issuance of MAS bills increased 2.7% q-o-q, accounting for almost 90% of total issuance in Q4 2024 (**Figure 3**). Treasury and other government bond issuance exhibited growth of 3.6% q-o-q in Q4 2024 on increased issuance of Treasury bills. Corporate bond issuance saw the fastest expansion among all LCY bond segments with 30.4% q-o-q growth. The largest corporate bond issuer in Q4 2024 was the Housing & Development Board as it issued bonds worth SGD2.3 billion, representing almost half of the LCY corporate issuance total during the quarter.

Figure 3: Composition of Local Currency Bond Issuance in Singapore

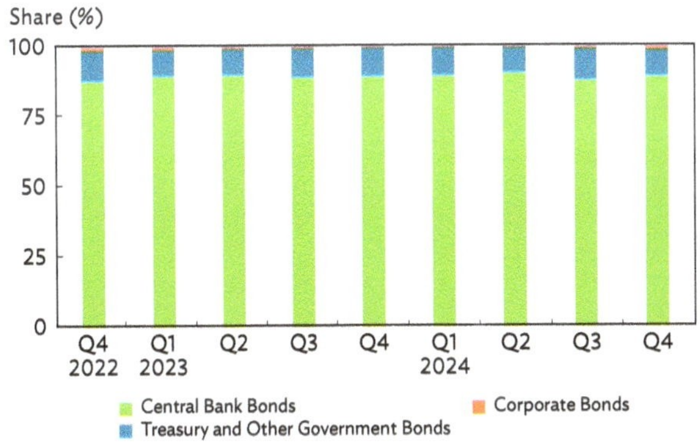

Q1 = first quarter, Q2 = second quarter, Q3 = third quarter, Q4 = fourth quarter.
Note: Corporate bonds are based on *AsianBondsOnline* estimates.
Sources: Monetary Authority of Singapore and Bloomberg LP.

Sustainable Bond Market

Singapore's sustainable bond market is dominated by green bond instruments, which accounted for 83.5% of the total at the end of December. Sustainable bonds outstanding reached USD26.0 billion at the end of Q4 2024, posting growth of 6.2% q-o-q (**Figure 4**). A majority (80.6%) of outstanding sustainable bonds were denominated in local currency. With bonds carrying maturities of over 5 years comprising 61.5% of total outstanding sustainable bonds, the size-weighted average tenor of sustainable bonds in Singapore stood at 16.7 years, the longest among emerging East Asian markets.[23] The largest issuer of sustainable bonds during the quarter was the state-owned Housing & Development Board, having issued 4-year fixed-rate green notes in October amounting to SGD900.0 million, or 44.3% of total quarterly issuance, to finance eligible green projects under its Green Finance Framework.

Figure 4: Market Profile of Outstanding Sustainable Bonds in Singapore at the End of December 2024

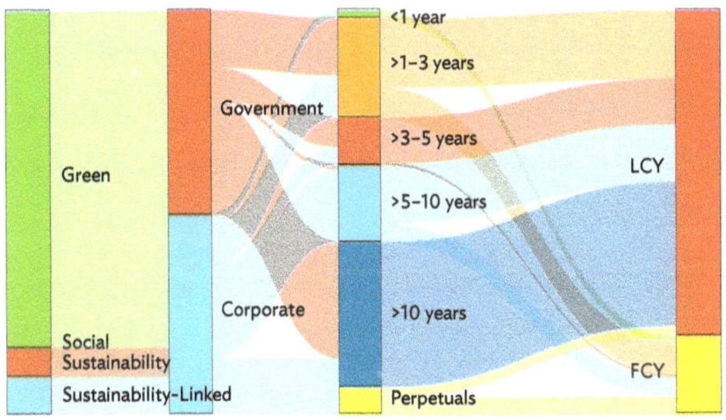

FCY = foreign currency, LCY = local currency.
Source: *AsianBondsOnline* calculations based on Bloomberg LP data.

[23] Emerging East Asia is defined to include member states of the Association of Southeast Asian Nations plus the People's Republic of China; Hong Kong, China; and the Republic of Korea.

Thailand

Yield Movements

Between 1 December 2024 and 28 February 2025, Thailand's local currency (LCY) government bond yields fell on the Bank of Thailand's (BOT) monetary policy easing amid weaker-than-expected economic performance. Yields declined an average of 12 basis points across all maturities following the BOT's decision to reduce its policy rate by 25 basis points to 2.00% during its 26 February meeting (**Figure 1**). The central bank cited weaker-than-expected economic growth and rising uncertainty from major economies' trade policies as reasons for the rate cut. Thailand's economy grew 3.2% year-on-year (y-o-y) in the fourth quarter (Q4) of 2024, up from 3.0% y-o-y in the previous quarter. Nonetheless, the full-year 2024 gross domestic product growth of 2.5% was below the BOT forecast of 2.7% and also among the slowest in emerging East Asia.[24]

Figure 1: Thailand's Benchmark Yield Curve—Local Currency Government Bonds

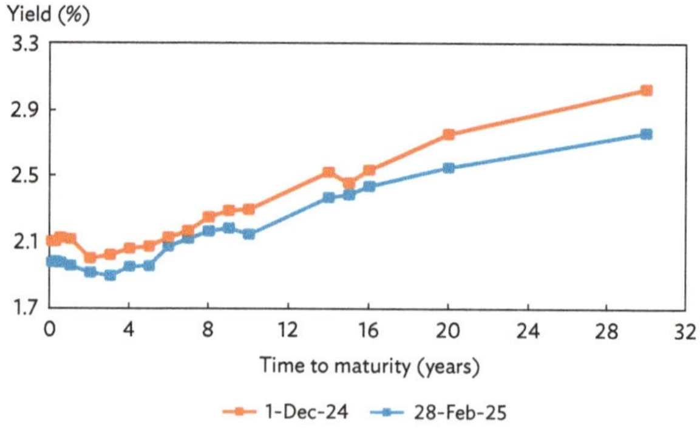

Sources: Based on data from Bloomberg LP and Thai Bond Market Association.

Local Currency Bond Market Size and Issuance

Thailand's LCY bond stock inched down in Q4 2024 due to contractions in corporate and BOT bonds. At the end of December, total LCY bonds outstanding amounted to THB17.1 trillion, down 0.1% quarter-on-quarter (q-o-q) (**Figure 2**). The stock of corporate bonds continued to decline, falling 1.6% q-o-q to THB4.6 trillion in Q4 2024 after contracting 1.8% q-o-q in the third quarter as investors remained cautious amid slow economic growth and rising uncertainties. BOT bonds outstanding also contracted 0.8% q-o-q to THB2.3 trillion in Q4 2024. Meanwhile, Treasury and other government bonds rose 0.8% q-o-q to THB10.1 trillion despite a contraction in issuance due to a relatively smaller volume of maturities.

Figure 2: Composition of Local Currency Bonds Outstanding in Thailand

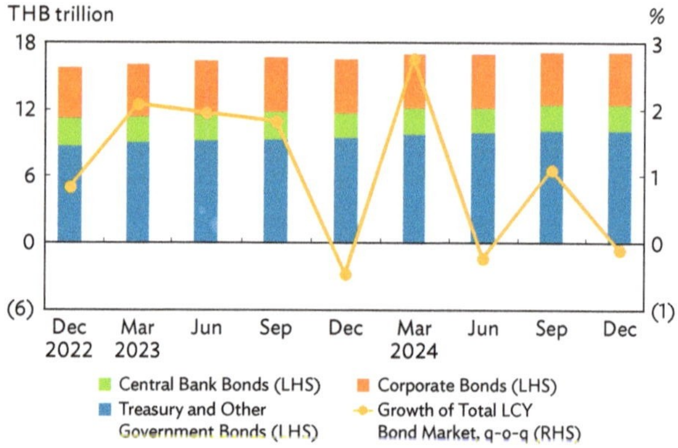

() = negative, LCY = local currency, LHS = left-hand side, q-o-q = quarter-on-quarter, RHS = right-hand side, THB = Thai baht.
Source: Bank of Thailand.

LCY bond issuance continued to decline in Q4 2024, dragged down by weak debt sales from both the public and private sectors. Total issuance of LCY bonds tallied THB2.1 trillion in Q4 2024, down 5.7% q-o-q after posting a 2.6% q-o-q contraction in the previous quarter (**Figure 3**). Treasury and other government bond issuance (THB602.3 billion) eased 9.4% q-o-q in Q4 2024 due in part to slightly smaller planned issuance of government bonds at the start of fiscal year 2025, which started in October. BOT issuance (THB1.1 trillion) posted a nominal 1.0% decline during the quarter. Corporate debt sales (THB346.2 billion) fell 13.2% q-o-q in Q4 2024 as investor confidence remained tepid amid downside risks to economic growth posed by the new United States

This market summary was written by Debbie Gundaya, consultant, Economic Research and Development Impact Department, Asian Development Bank, Manila.

[24] Emerging East Asia is defined to include member states of the Association of Southeast Asian Nations plus the People's Republic of China; Hong Kong, China; and the Republic of Korea.

Figure 3: Composition of Local Currency Bond Issuance in Thailand

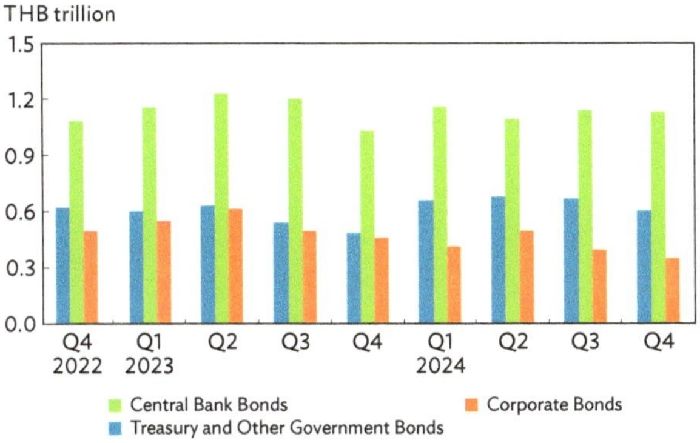

Q1 = first quarter, Q2 = second quarter, Q3 = third quarter, Q4 = fourth quarter, THB = Thai baht.

Source: Bank of Thailand.

administration's trade policies. Siam Cement was the top corporate issuer in Q4 2024 with total bond sales amounting to THB40.0 billion, representing 11.6% of total corporate issuance during the quarter.

Investor Profile

Domestic investors' holdings of LCY government bonds increased. Holdings of domestic investors rose to 90.7% of total LCY government bonds at the end of December, up from 89.3% a year earlier (**Figure 4**). Meanwhile, foreign holdings fell to 9.3% from 10.7% during the same period as weak economic performance and global uncertainties capped demand for Thai government bonds.

Figure 4: Investor Profile of Government Bonds in Thailand

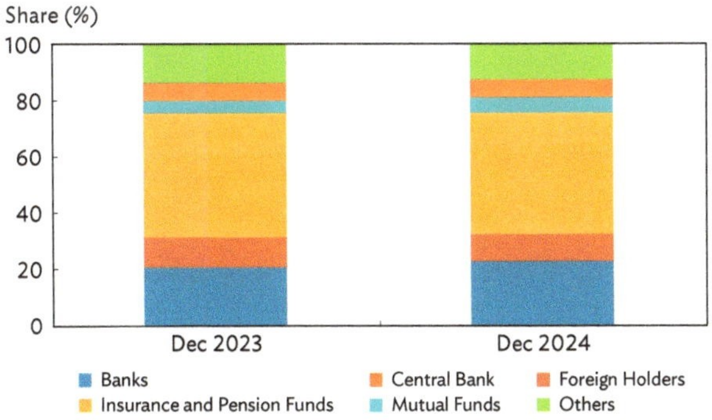

Source: Bank of Thailand.

Sustainable Bond Market

Thailand's sustainable bonds are predominantly instruments issued by the public sector. Thailand's sustainable bond market grew 6.3% q-o-q and 18.1% y-o-y to reach a size of USD24.1 billion at the end of December. Sustainability bonds (USD15.8 billion) comprised a majority of sustainable instruments, accounting for 65.6% of the market (**Figure 5**). Green bonds (USD4.4 billion) followed, with an 18.4% share of total sustainable bonds. Over two-thirds of outstanding sustainable bonds were government-issued instruments, which typically have longer maturities. Nearly 90% of outstanding government sustainable bonds had remaining maturities of longer than 10 years. As a result, the size-weighted average tenor of outstanding sustainable bonds in Thailand was among the longest in the region at 8.9 years. Over 98% of sustainable bonds in Thailand were denominated in local currency, which remained the highest share among all emerging East Asian markets.

Figure 5: Market Profile of Outstanding Sustainable Bonds in Thailand at the End of December 2024

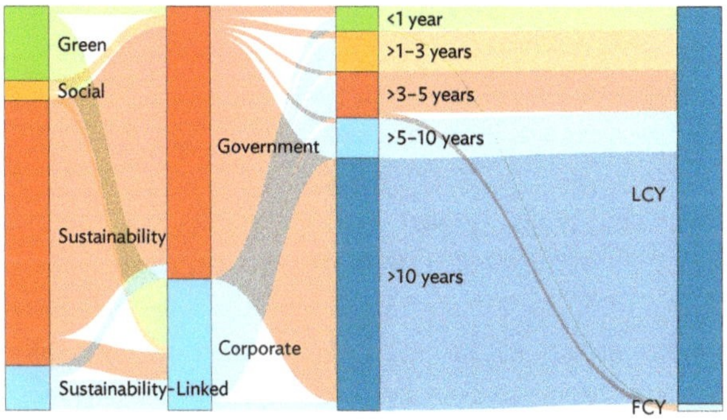

FCY = foreign currency, LCY = local currency.

Source: *AsianBondsOnline* calculations based on Bloomberg LP data.

Viet Nam

Yield Movements

Between 1 December 2024 and 28 February 2025, the local currency (LCY) sovereign bond yield curve in Viet Nam shifted upward. Yields climbed an average of 34 basis points across all maturities, propelled by strong economic growth (**Figure 1**). Viet Nam's economy grew the fastest among its emerging East Asian peers, expanding 7.1% in full-year 2024—fueled by strong exports and investments—and surpassing the government's target growth of 6.5%.[25] On 19 February, the National Assembly raised its economic growth target for full-year 2025 to at least 8.0% from an initial target of 6.5%–7.0% in November. Furthermore, the uptick in yields was also influenced by uncertainties over the path of global economic policies.

Figure 1: Viet Nam's Benchmark Yield Curve—Local Currency Government Bonds

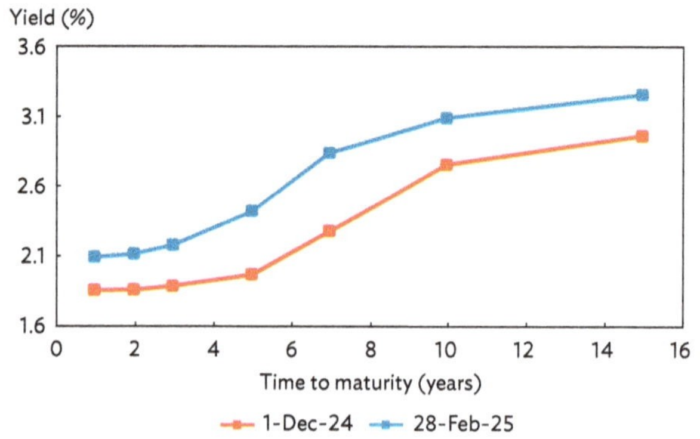

Source: Based on data from Bloomberg LP.

Local Currency Bond Market Size and Issuance

Expansion in all bond segments buoyed the LCY bond market's growth in the fourth quarter (Q4) of 2024. Despite reduced issuance from all bond segments, total LCY bond market growth accelerated to 5.0% quarter-on-quarter (q-o-q) in Q4 2024 due to the reduced volume of maturing bonds (**Figure 2**). Outstanding Treasury and other government bonds reached VND2,220.4 trillion at the end of December on growth of 2.3% q-o-q, slower than the previous quarter's 5.3% q-o-q growth. Similarly, the total corporate debt stock totaled VND803.1 trillion at the end of December on slower growth of 4.4% q-o-q, following an 8.3% q-o-q expansion in the third quarter. Meanwhile, the stock of central bank securities jumped 95.0% q-o-q in Q4 2024, reversing the previous quarter's contraction of 52.6% q-o-q.

Figure 2: Composition of Local Currency Bonds Outstanding in Viet Nam

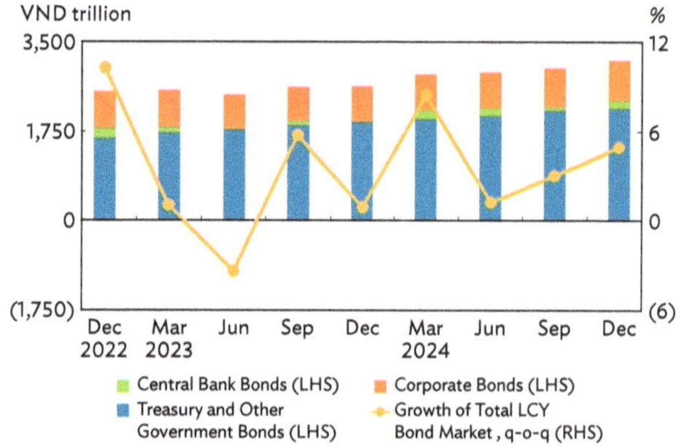

( ) = negative, LCY = local currency, LHS = left-hand side, q-o-q = quarter-on-quarter, RHS = right-hand side, VND = Vietnamese dong.

Note: Other government bonds comprise government-guaranteed and municipal bonds.

Sources: Hanoi Stock Exchange, State Bank of Vietnam, Vietnam Bond Market Association, and Bloomberg LP.

LCY bond issuance contracted 6.0% q-o-q in Q4 2024 on reduced debt sale across all bond types. Issuance of Treasury and other government bonds fell 49.0% q-o-q in Q4 2024 due to the government largely meeting its required annual borrowing in the previous quarters (**Figure 3**). Similarly, corporate bond issuance dropped 1.7% q-o-q in Q4 2024, driven by a slowdown in issuance in the corporate market's leading sector (banking) after banks had met the prudential ratios set by the State Bank of Vietnam in the prior quarter. The banking and property sectors remained the key drivers of issuance in Viet Nam's LCY corporate bond market, accounting for 55.1% and 22.7%, respectively, of the corporate issuance total in Q4 2024. During the quarter, IDI International Development and Investment Corporation and

This market summary was written by Jeremy Grace Ilustrisimo, consultant, Economic Research and Development Impact Department, Asian Development Bank, Manila.

[25] Emerging East Asia is defined to include member states of the Association of Southeast Asian Nations plus the People's Republic of China; Hong Kong, China; and the Republic of Korea.

Figure 3: Composition of Local Currency Bond Issuance in Viet Nam

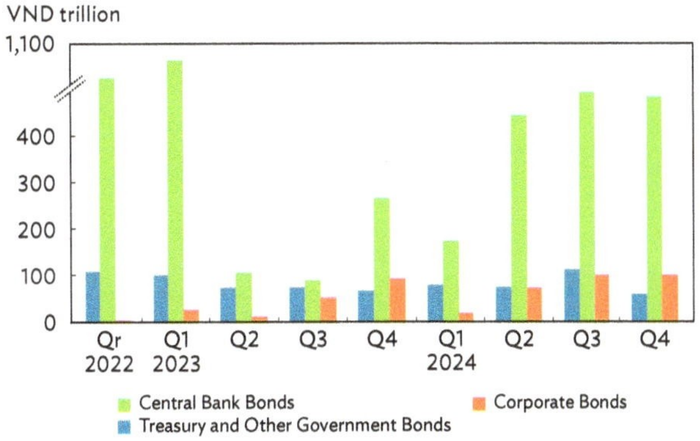

Q1 = first quarter, Q2 = second quarter, Q3 = third quarter, Q4 = fourth quarter, VND = Vietnamese dong.

Note: Other government bonds comprise government-guaranteed and municipal bonds.

Sources: Hanoi Stock Exchange, State Bank of Vietnam, Vietnam Bond Market Association, and Bloomberg LP.

Figure 4: Profile of the Two Dominant Investors for Local Currency Government Bonds

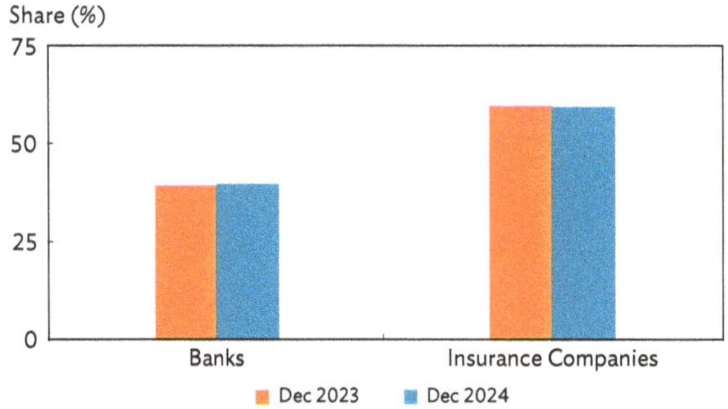

Source: Ministry of Finance, Viet Nam.

Figure 5: Market Profile of Outstanding Sustainable Bonds in Viet Nam at the End of December 2024

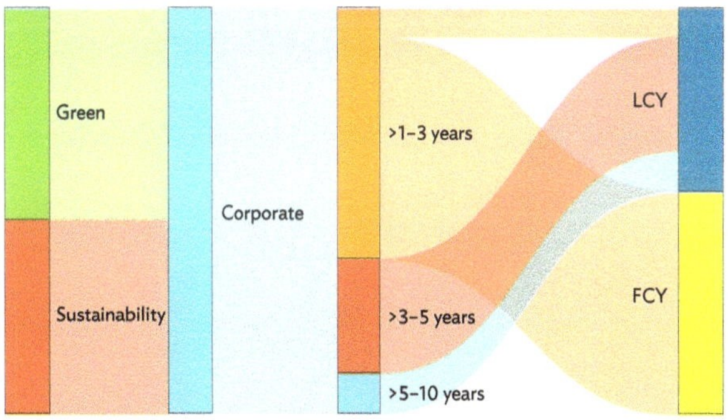

FCY = foreign currency, LCY = local currency.

Source: *AsianBondsOnline* calculations based on Bloomberg LP data.

Vietcombank issued green bonds worth VND1.0 trillion and VND2.0 trillion, respectively. The largest corporate issuance during the quarter came from HD Bank, with total debt sales of VND9.0 trillion, representing 8.8% of the total corporate bond issuance during the quarter.

Investor Profile

At the end of December, the investor landscape in the LCY government bond market remained largely unchanged from a year earlier. Viet Nam's LCY government bond market remained dominated by only two investor groups—insurance firms and banks—with a combined holdings share of 99.2% in December 2024, a slight dip from the previous year's 99.4% (**Figure 4**). The heavy concentration of investments from just two investor groups resulted in Viet Nam earning the highest Herfindahl-Hirschman Index score among its regional peers at the end of December.[26]

Sustainable Bond Market

The private sector remained the sole player in Viet Nam's sustainable bond market, which mainly comprises green and sustainability instruments carrying short-term tenors. Green and sustainability bonds accounted for a nearly equal share of the market with shares of 52.2% and 47.8%, respectively, of the total sustainable debt stock at the end of Q4 2024 (**Figure 5**). Total outstanding sustainable bonds grew 11.6% q-o-q to reach USD1.1 billion at the end of December, up from USD1.0 billion in the previous quarter. More than 50.0% of the total sustainable debt stock was in the form of foreign-currency-denominated bonds, while over 60.0% of sustainable bonds carried tenors of 3 years or less, resulting in a size-weighted average tenor of 2.9 years at the end of Q4 2024, among the shortest in the region. On 4 December, Techcombank voluntarily launched its Green Bond Framework, making a pioneering move as the first private bank in Viet Nam to advance toward sustainability. Furthermore, IDI International Development and Investment Corporation's green bond issuance in October marked the first green bond from the agriculture sector.

[26] The Herfindahl-Hirschman Index is a common measure of market concentration. The index is used to measure the investor profile diversification of the local currency bond market by summing the squared share of each investor group in the bond market.

www.ingramcontent.com/pod-product-compliance
Lightning Source LLC
Chambersburg PA
CBHW041801220926
51847CB00014B/275
9789292772543